978191331606 8

AF064045

LONDON
RAVE FLYERS
1990 - 1996

For Matt Acornley

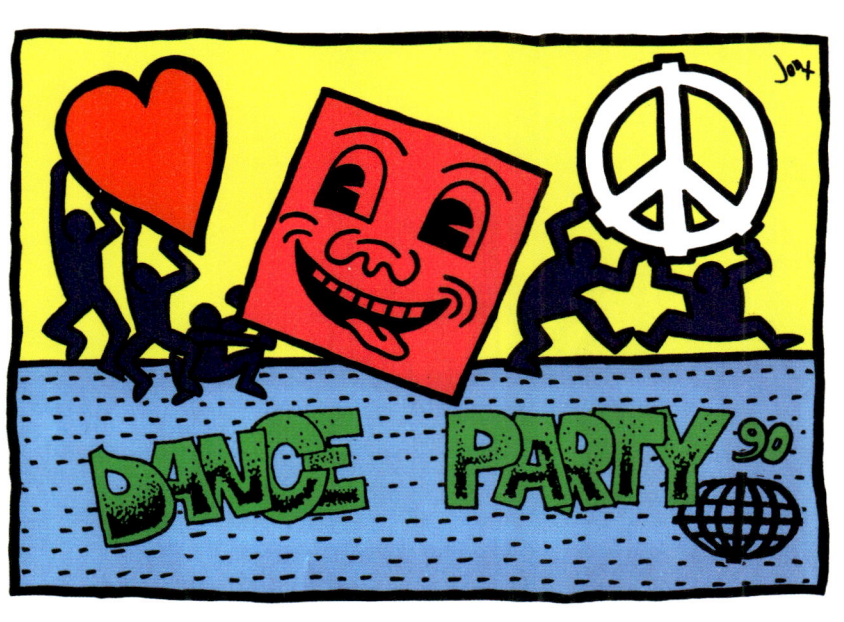

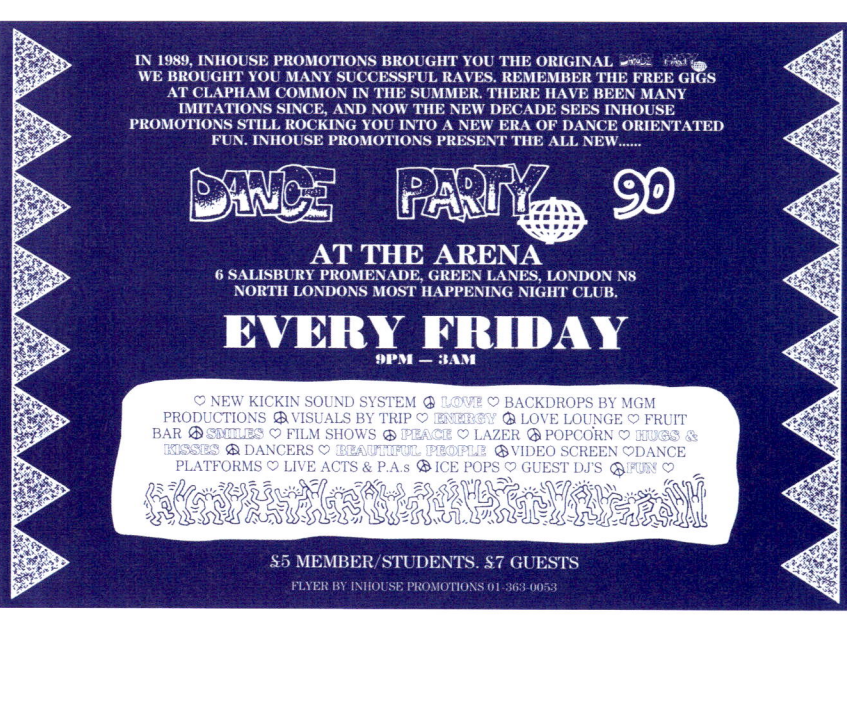

IN 1989, INHOUSE PROMOTIONS BROUGHT YOU THE ORIGINAL ⬛ ⬛
WE BROUGHT YOU MANY SUCCESSFUL RAVES. REMEMBER THE FREE GIGS
AT CLAPHAM COMMON IN THE SUMMER. THERE HAVE BEEN MANY
IMITATIONS SINCE, AND NOW THE NEW DECADE SEES INHOUSE
PROMOTIONS STILL ROCKING YOU INTO A NEW ERA OF DANCE ORIENTATED
FUN. INHOUSE PROMOTIONS PRESENT THE ALL NEW......

DANCE PARTY 90

AT THE ARENA
6 SALISBURY PROMENADE, GREEN LANES, LONDON N8
NORTH LONDONS MOST HAPPENING NIGHT CLUB.

EVERY FRIDAY
9PM – 3AM

♡ NEW KICKIN SOUND SYSTEM ☮ LOVE ♡ BACKDROPS BY MGM
PRODUCTIONS ☮ VISUALS BY TRIP ♡ ENERGY ☮ LOVE LOUNGE ♡ FRUIT
BAR ☮ SMILES ♡ FILM SHOWS ☮ PEACE ♡ LAZER ☮ POPCORN ♡ HUGS &
KISSES ☮ DANCERS ♡ BEAUTIFUL PEOPLE ☮ VIDEO SCREEN ♡ DANCE
PLATFORMS ♡ LIVE ACTS & P.A.s ☮ ICE POPS ♡ GUEST DJ'S ☮ FUN ♡

£5 MEMBER/STUDENTS. £7 GUESTS

FLYER BY INHOUSE PROMOTIONS 01-363-0053

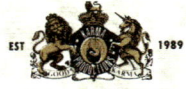

KARMA PRODUCTIONS
PRESENT

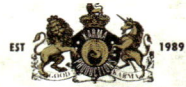

E N E R G Y

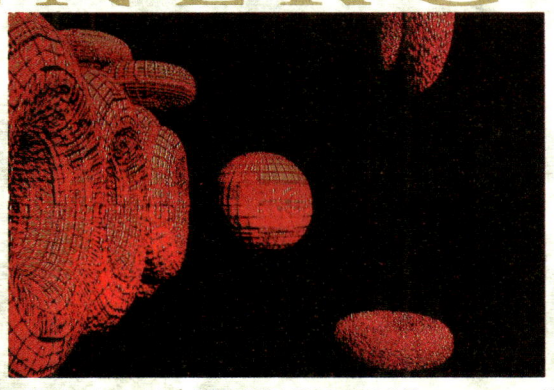

On SATURDAY, 20th JANUARY, 1990 From 9pm till 6am.
At The Academy Theatre, 211 Stockwell Road, Brixton, London SW9

LIVE ACTS - THE K.L.F. AND GURU JOSH

GUESTS *from NEW YORK - FRANKIE BONES · TOMMY MUSTO*

DJ's - MIKE PICKERING · FABIO · FRANKY FONCETT · CARL COX · TREVOR FUNG PLUS OTHER DJ's

This will be our first event of 1990 in which we will be using a top line up of DJ's from London as well as our guest DJ's Frankie Bones and Tommy Musto from New York. But we aren't just using DJ's. We will also have the KLF and the Really mad Guru Josh both making live appearances exclusively at Energy. As always the Karma team will be decorating to a high standard as well as our new lazer systems and full vari-lite show. You are assured many surprise effects and entertainments to make this event unique. Unfortunately, tickets do sell out for each event and we urge you to purchase early to avoid disappointment.

TICKETS

£19 before Friday, 19th January, £21 afterwards - For members £17 before and £19 after (members receive discount at little empire)

MEMBERSHIP

Many of you will have already received an official membership card. This will enable you to buy tickets at a reduced price, but the reduction is only available at our shop "Little Empire" in Fulham. If you would like to become a member, the latest we can accept membership applications is up to 24 hours before the start of the event. Members are allowed to purchase tickets for a limited number of guests.

GENERAL INFORMATION NUMBER FOR ALL ENQUIRIES: 0860 013542(24 HOURS)
FOR URGENT ENQUIRIES, NOT GENERAL INFO. CALL: 01- 736 6390 OR 01- 384 2060.

TICKET AGENTS

PAUL & DAVE 01 674 3287 BRIXTON	SIMON 01-223 8420 BATTERSEA	MARK 0932 568976 CHERTSEY
ALAN 0836 336089 WEMBLEY	RICK 0705 811341 PORTSMOUTH	ROBERT 0462 49361b NORTH HERTS
MAXIMI 0273 2765 BRIGHTON	CHRIS 0727 32232 ST. ALBANS	FINBAR 01-906 2283 NORTH
NICK 0276 35958 SURREY	WARREN 01-518 0086 ILFORD	GODWIN 0831 401159 WINDSOR SOUTH

TICKET OUTLETS

MAIN TICKET OUTLET: *LITTLE EMPIRE (ENERGY SHOP) 19b JERDAN PLACE, FULHAM BROADWAY, SW6*
(BUY 12 RECEIVE 1 FREE ONLY AT THIS OUTLET.) 01- 386 5964.

BLACK MARKET RECORDS 25 D'ARBLAY STREET, SOHO. W1 01-437 0478
BEGGARS BANQUET 62 EDEN STREET KINGSTON. 01-549 5871

MUSIC STATION. THE BASEMENT. KEN MARKET, KENSINGTON 0836 336089
WORLDCLASS RECORDS 18 CHURCH WALK, COLCHESTER ESSEX 0206 768979

NOTE FOR NOTE RECORDS CENTRAL PARADE HOW E ST. WALTHAMSTOWE E17 01-521 4223
MUSIC POWER RECORDS 37 GRAND PARADE, GREEN LANES. HARRINGAY N4 01 800 6113
PASSION RECORDS 71 OXFORD ST. W1 01-434 4669

☞ Knowledge
Wednesday 28 Feb
JiMi POLO LiVe
& DJ Graeme Park

The Brain Club
11 Wardour Street W1
STOP

DUNGEON

THE DATE: **SAT 24TH FEB**
THE VENUE: **LEA BRIDGE RD, E10**

THE DJ's

FABIO

ELLIS DEE

GROOVE RIDER

MATTHE B

CHALKY WHITE

PLEASE DO NOT PARK
ON LEA BRIDGE RD
ARRIVE EARLY TO ENSURE ENTRY

Printed by CLEARAPRINT. Tel 01-241 2910

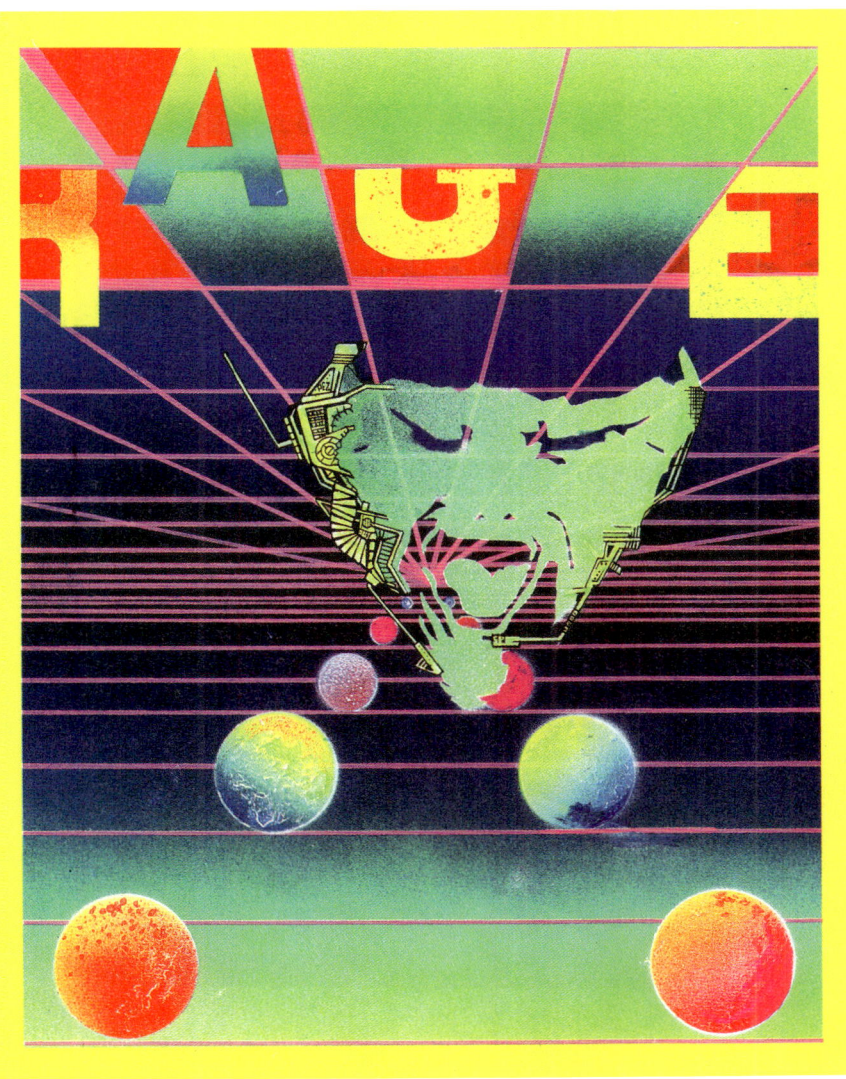

RAGE

At Heaven Under the Arches WC2 on
Thursday 1st March

DJs: Colin Faver·Trevor Fung
Groove Rider·Fabio·Craig Grant·Phuze

All the dance space you need to the best sound system around and
state of the art lazers with stunning back up lights.
Plus relaxing Lol lounge.

ATTENTION!

RAGE is now a members only club.
NO MEMBERSHIP NO ADMISSION
SO GET ONE !!!

For details of membership call 839 5458 or visit
2nd floor office, 34 Craven St. WC2 (Next to Heaven)
Monday-Friday 10.30-6.30

Admission Five Pounds before 11.00 or
Six Pounds before 11.30 with this invitation

CARNIVAL 90

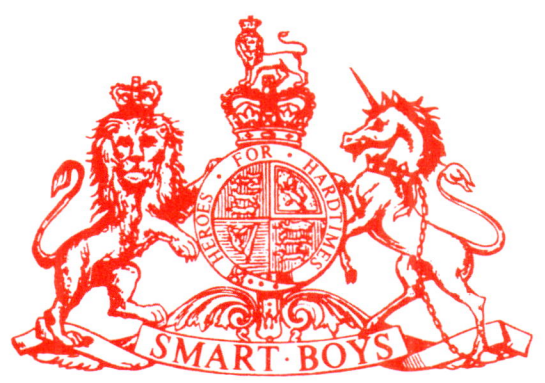

SPONSORED BY GAP

SUNDAY 26TH AUGUST
MONDAY 27TH AUGUST
12 AM. - 7.00 PM.

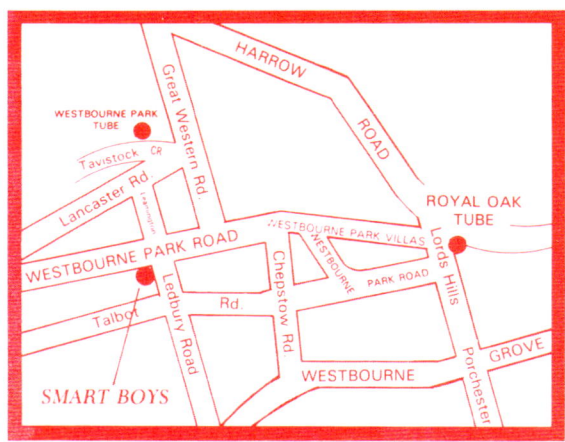

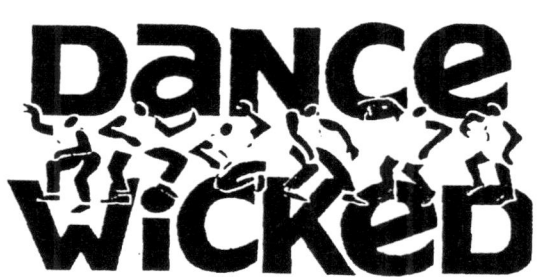

CLOSING
PARTY

SATURDAY 11th MAY
at
THE ARCH
66 GODING STREET
LONDON SE11

Featuring the
Dance Wicked DJ^s

10pm ~ Late

£7   £5 Members

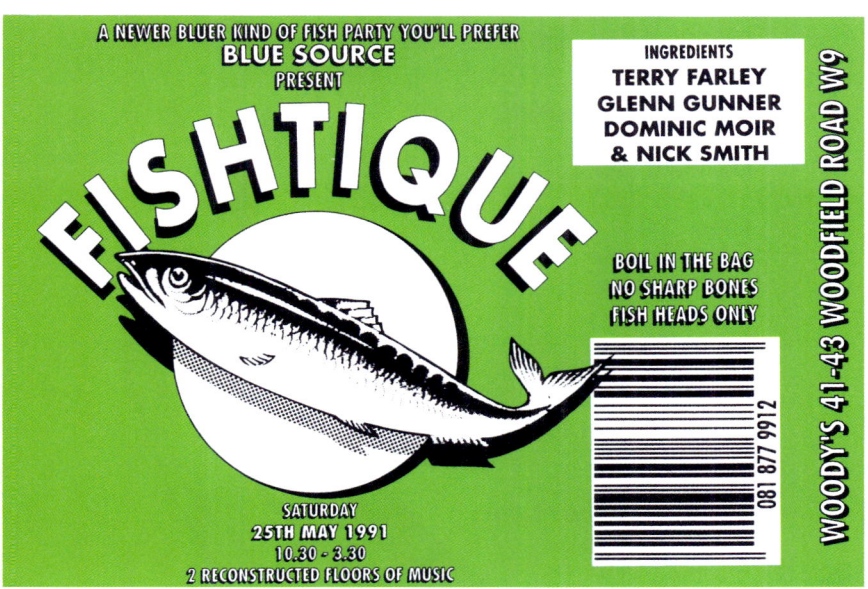

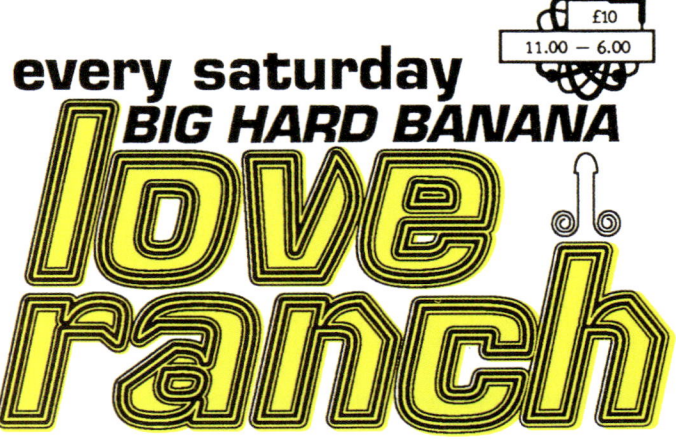

every saturday
BIG HARD BANANA
love
ranch

£10
11.00 – 6.00

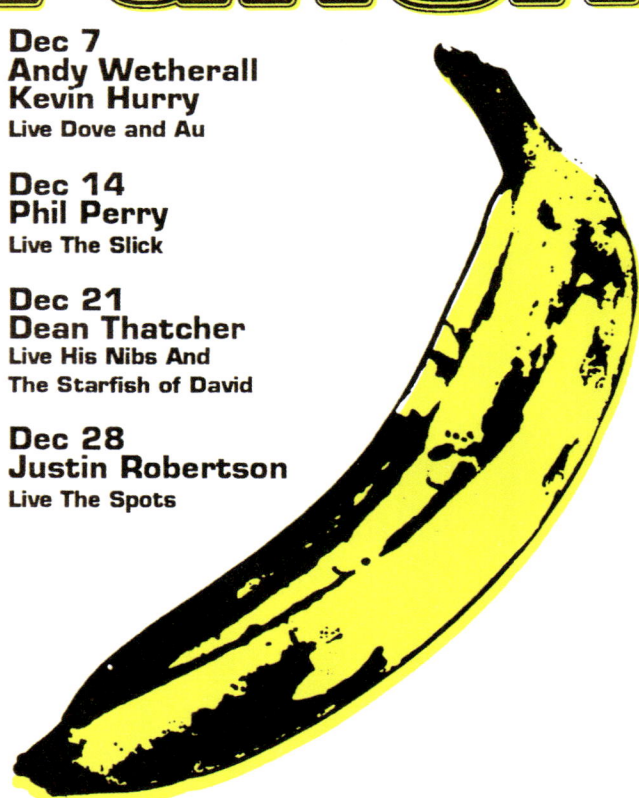

Dec 7
Andy Wetherall
Kevin Hurry
Live Dove and Au

Dec 14
Phil Perry
Live The Slick

Dec 21
Dean Thatcher
Live His Nibs And
The Starfish of David

Dec 28
Justin Robertson
Live The Spots

plus residential DJ's Al Mackenzie Rad Rice

11.00 – 6.00
Maximus
14 Leicester Square

SPRING DANCE PARTY
FRIDAY | 3rd MAY

1991

IS ANYBODY THERE?
10pm - 6am

VISION ON

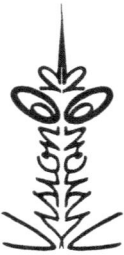

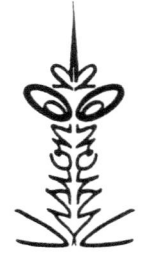

FRIDAY 3rd MAY
10pm - 6am

In 1989, we brought you one of the best and most talked about raves in Central London. Now the time has come once again to rekindle your desire to have a wild and wicked time. Vision On.

Turntable Technicians:
CARL "III DEX" COX   GROOVE RIDER
ELLIS DEE   RM   TIN-TIN
GUEST DJ SUBJECT 13
LIVE ON STAGE - LUNARCI
LIVE ON STAGE - SUBJECT 13
To add versatility to the visual element we have
BACKDROPS AND PROPS. 3D MOVIES
DELIRIOUS LIGHTING
MULTI-COLOUR LASERS
WITH MANY MORE EFFECTS
ART BY MIYUKI & FUKUMI OF ZUBO
JUICE, COCKTAILS AND ALCOHOL AVAILABLE
Tickets £12.50 Advance - More On The Door

VENUE - THE ROCKET
166-220 HOLLOWAY ROAD N7
FOR TICKET OUTLETS & MORE INFORMATION

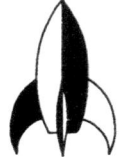

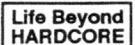

0898 88 66 26

33p off peak, 44p peak

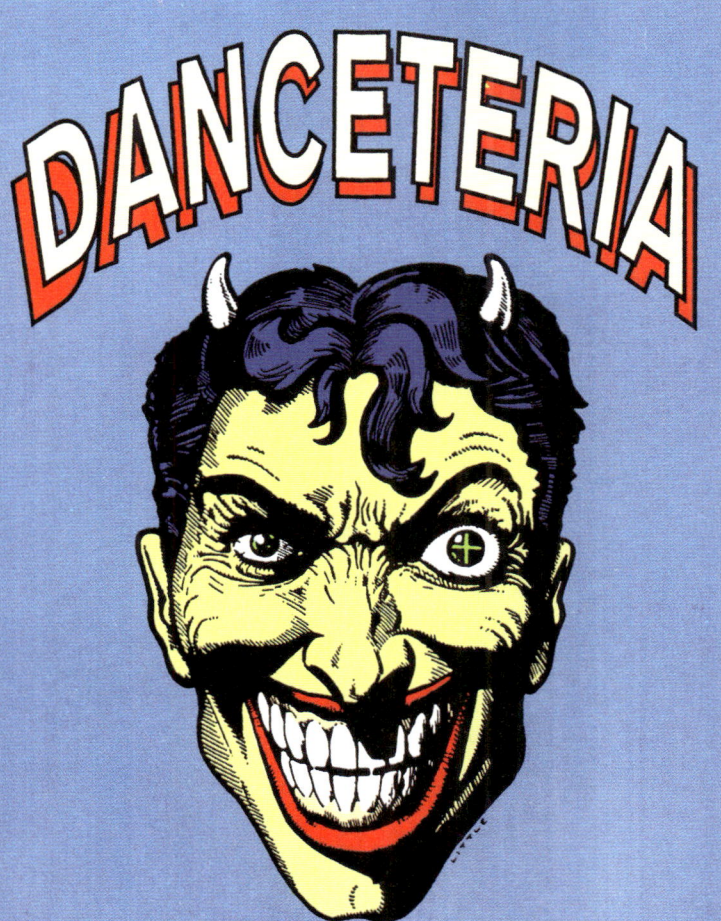

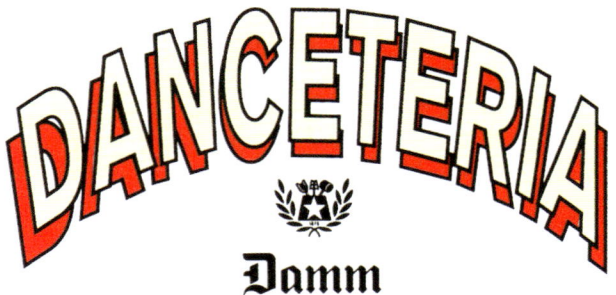

DANCETERIA

Damm

FRIDAY
10TH JULY
AND EVERY FRIDAY ONWARDS
DJ'S
NORMAN JAY
TERRY FARLEY
STEVE LEE
SCOTT & DANNY MAC
STEVE SAVVA
ROCKY & DIESEL
STEVE BUTLER
SUDGE
10PM - 3.30AM
£10

LIMELIGHT
136 SHAFTSBURY AVE W1

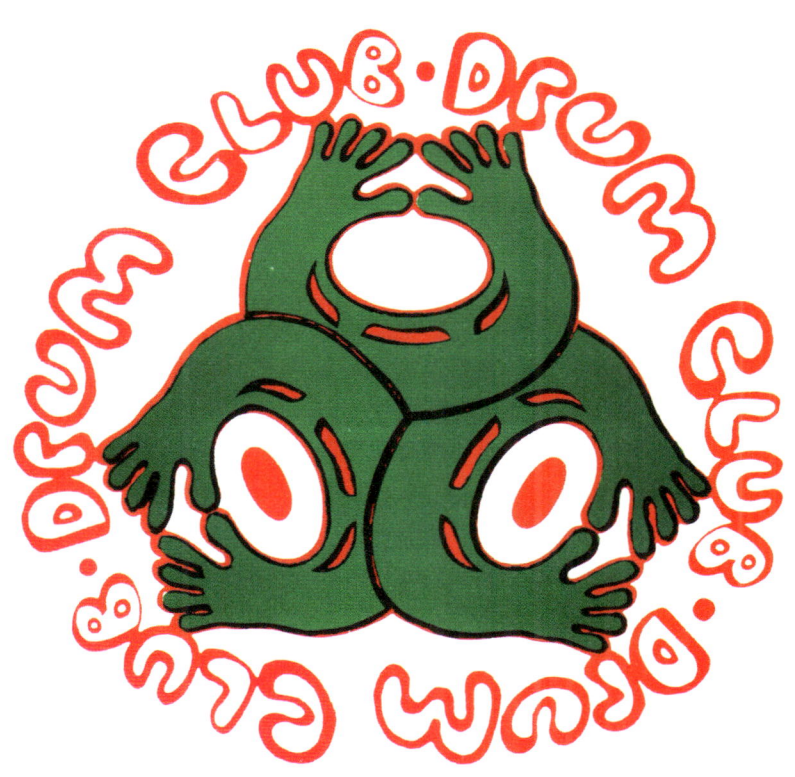

THE
DRUM CLUB

THE SOUND SHAFT (behind Heaven)
CRAVEN STREET, LONDON WC2

THURSDAY 17th DECEMBER
Simon Cross
PHIL PERRY
DIGS & WOOSH (DIY)

XMAS EVE PARTY (NORMAL ADMISSION PRICE!)
Red Marc
FABIO PARAS
LAWRENCE NELSON

NEW YEARS EVE PARTY
(AT A SECRET CENTRAL LONDON VENUE)
DARREN EMERSON BILLY NASTY
SCOTT JAMES CHARLIE HALL
CALL FOR DETAILS 0N 071 713 0053

THURSDAY 7th JANUARY
Ian James
ANDY WEATHERALL
CHARLIE HALL

£6/£4 members, students & £5 with this invite
" trancey, tribal house in a rub-a-dub style!!!"

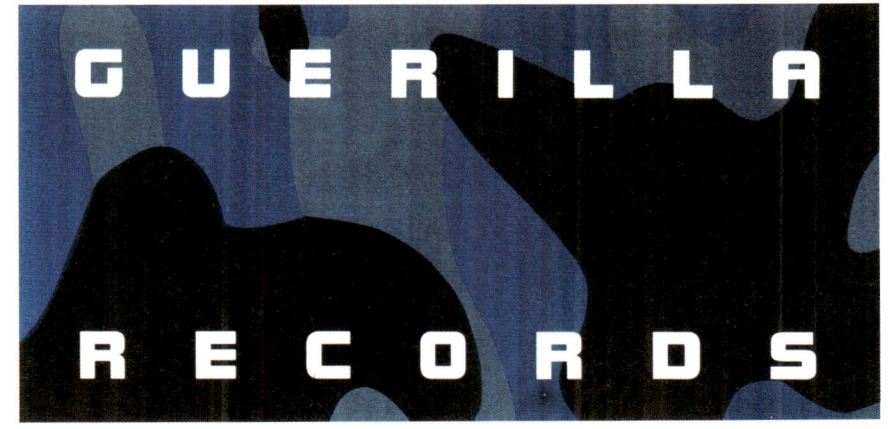

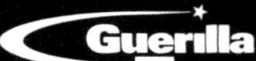

DUB HOUSE
DISCO

THE SECOND
ANNUAL GUERILLA RECORDS
BIRTHDAY PARTY
FRIDAY 13TH NOVEMBER AT ICENI
11 WHITEHORSE ST. MAYFAIR
LONDON W1 10.30PM - 3.30 AM

Featuring:

DARREN EMERSON
LISA LOUD
KEVIN HURRY &
KEVIN SWAIN (D.O.P)
PAUL DALEY
MICHAEL KILKIE
SCOTT JAMES
Live- SUPEREAL

TICKETS £12 FROM ZOOM, FLYING + TAG.
ANY REMAINING TICKETS ON DOOR ON NIGHT, FIRST COME, FIRST SERVED!
Come Early!! Limited Capacity.

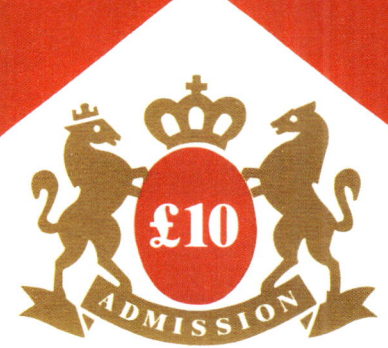

OCEANS, GOSWELL RD, EC1

£10 ADMISSION

Excellent!

Saturday 28th November (10pm-4.30am)

SMOKIN'JO · DAVE LAMBERT
CAD · DARREN BURTON

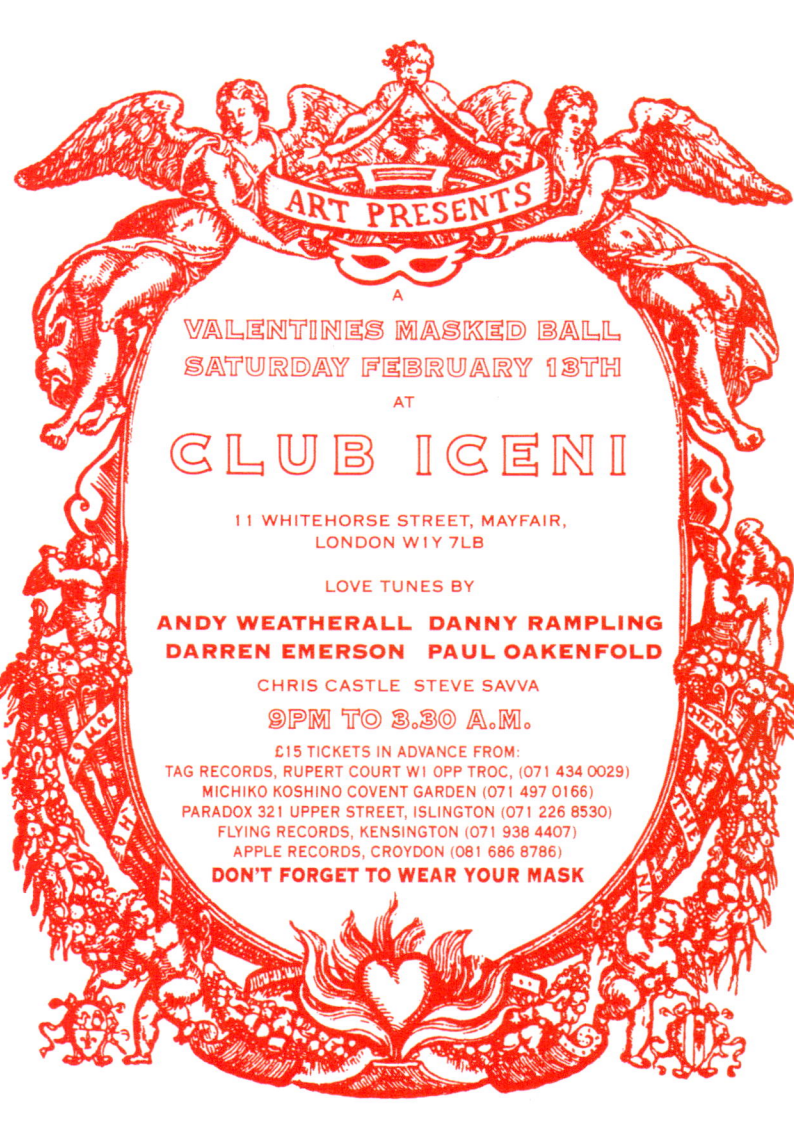

ART PRESENTS

A

VALENTINES MASKED BALL
SATURDAY FEBRUARY 13TH

AT

CLUB ICENI

11 WHITEHORSE STREET, MAYFAIR,
LONDON W1Y 7LB

LOVE TUNES BY

**ANDY WEATHERALL   DANNY RAMPLING
DARREN EMERSON   PAUL OAKENFOLD**

CHRIS CASTLE STEVE SAVVA

9PM TO 3.30 A.M.

£15 TICKETS IN ADVANCE FROM:
TAG RECORDS, RUPERT COURT W1 OPP TROC, (071 434 0029)
MICHIKO KOSHINO COVENT GARDEN (071 497 0166)
PARADOX 321 UPPER STREET, ISLINGTON (071 226 8530)
FLYING RECORDS, KENSINGTON (071 938 4407)
APPLE RECORDS, CROYDON (081 686 8786)
DON'T FORGET TO WEAR YOUR MASK

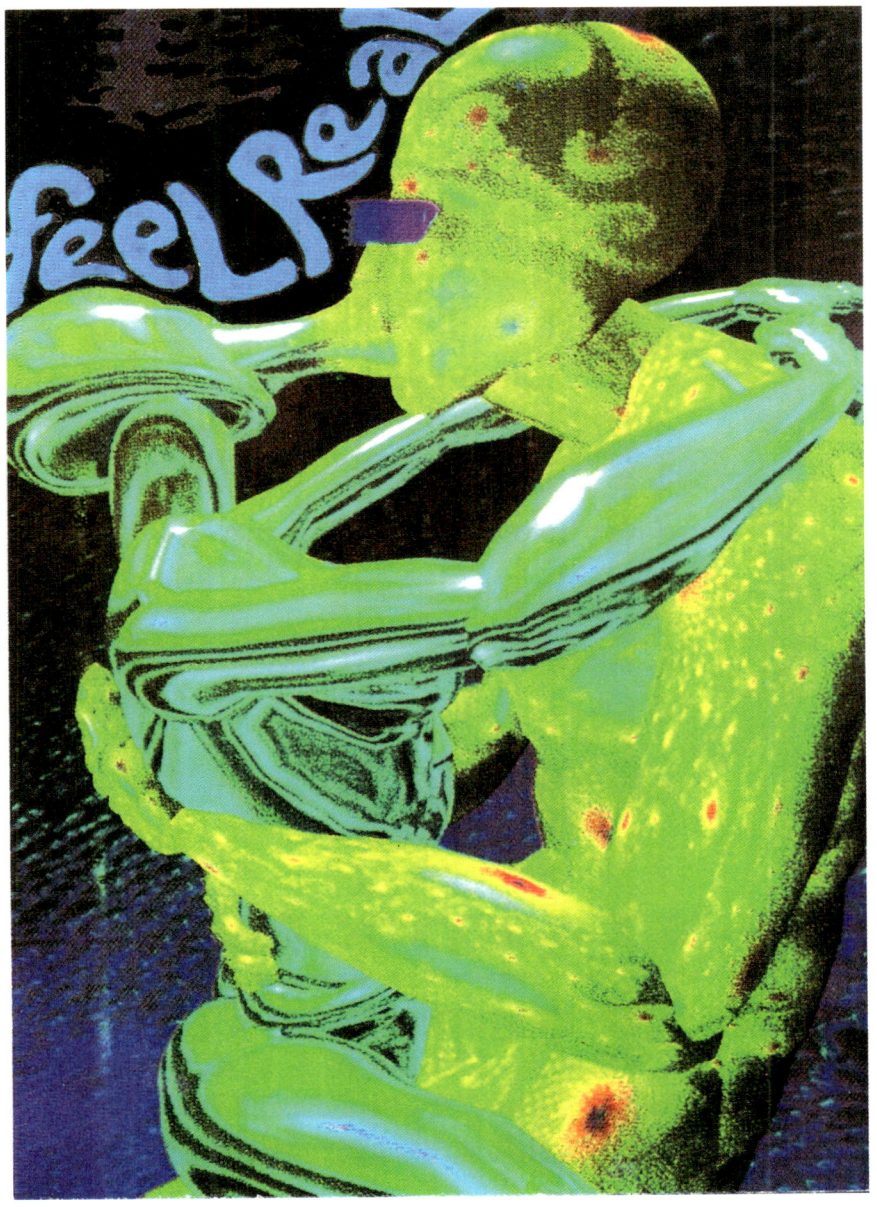

EVERY FRIDAY
11pm-6am
DEEP AND GROOVY HOUSE

OCTOBER 16TH

EDDIE RICHARDS · SUMI
RHYTHM DR · ROB ACTESON

OCTOBER 23RD

EVIL OLIVE · RHYTHM DR
ROB ACTESON · FEMI B

PLUS SUPER M.C'S
E-MIX & MYSTIC AURRA

AT THE GARDENING CLUB
THE PIAZZA COVENT GARDEN

PRESENTED BY THE UK HOUSE AUTHORITY

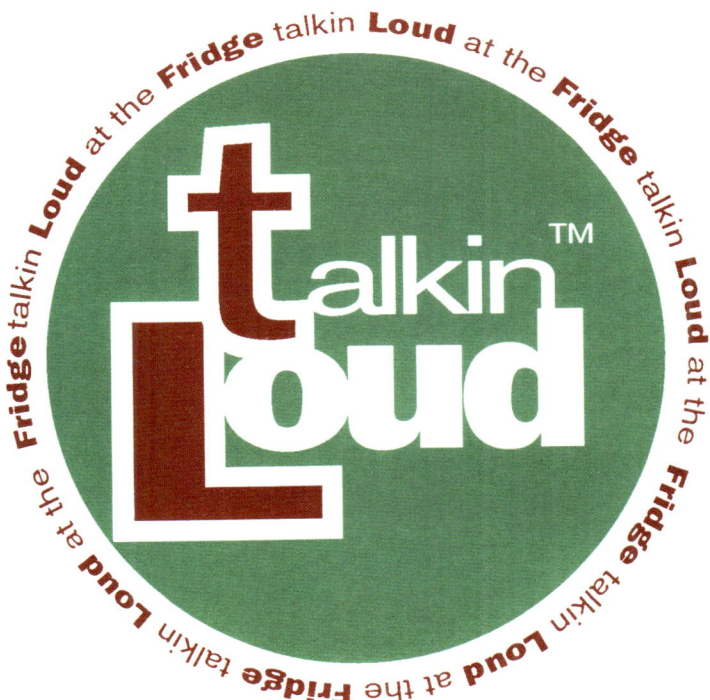

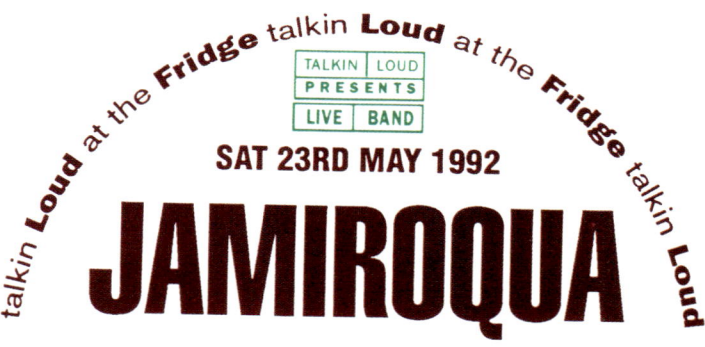

talkin **Loud** at the **Fridge** talkin **Loud** at the **Fridge** talkin **Loud**

TALKIN | LOUD
PRESENTS
LIVE | BAND

SAT 23RD MAY 1992

JAMIROQUA

10.00pm - 3.30am

© 1992 Swifty Typographics

Talkin Loud
At the Fridge/London
(Town Hall Parade, Brixton Hill SW2)
Every Saturday £8.00
£6 with flyer before 11pm/£5 after 2am
DJ's Gilles Peterson
Patrick Forge
+ Guests

Fridge at the Fridge talkin **Loud** at the **Fridge** talkin **Loud** at the **Fridge** talkin **Loud** at the **Fridge**

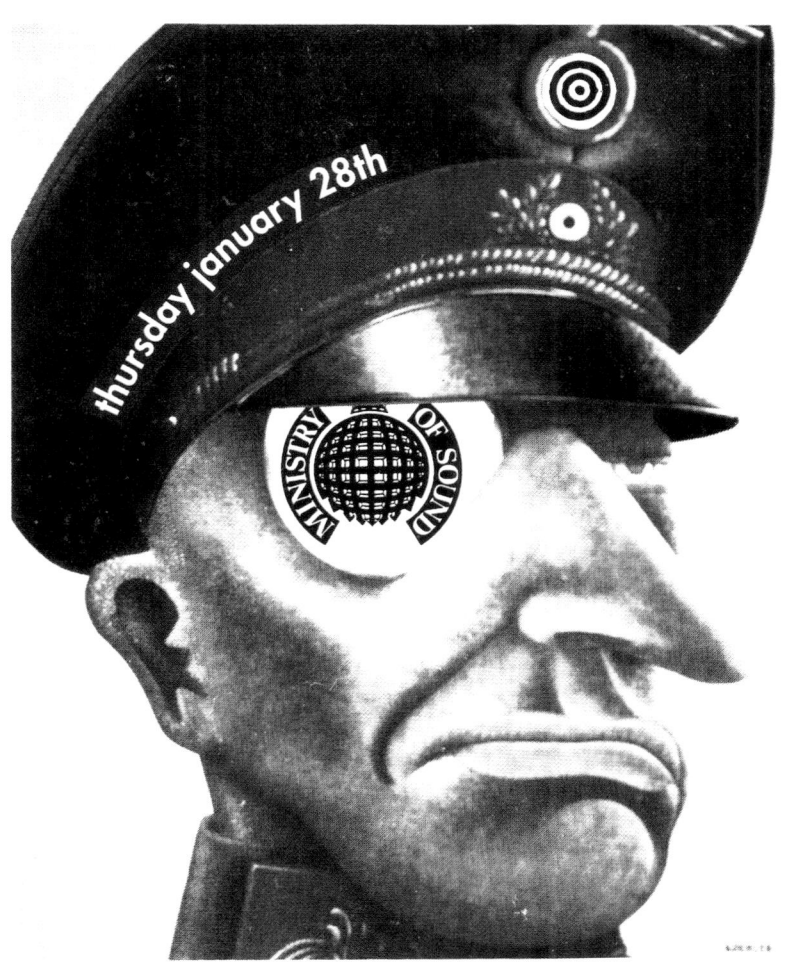

achtung

Achtung!

THURSDAY 28TH JANUARY

Ein zusammentreffen gleichgesinnter menschen aus der ganzen welt,
im streben die bewegung des Techno weiterzuführen. Um ein mekka
zu bilden für alle anhanger purer Techno Musik, wo man andere
anhanger treffen kann um sich völlig seinen traumen und wunschen
hinzugeben in einer unvergleichlichen atmosphare!

Module One

WESTBAM
DERRICK MAY
COLIN FAVER STEVE BICKNELL

Module Two

IN THE AREA FROM *SPIRAL TRIBE*
JOSH & AZTEC

Plus Guests

TREVOR ROCKCLIFFE
DAZ SAUND   DOMINIC

Module Three

FAT CAT RECORDS PARTY

With

ALEX KNIGHT
MIXMASTER MORRIS
JOSE' (CAFE DEL MAR)

Plus Interactive Erotic Industrial Cabaret from

HIVE

OPEN 10pm - 6am
ADMISSION £8, £4 after 3am
MoS, 103 Gaunt Street, London SE1 071 378 6528
Over 21's only. I.D. Required

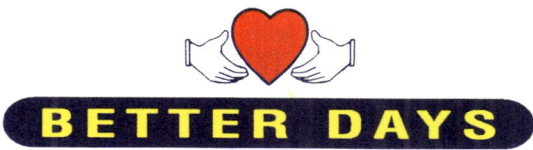

BETTER DAYS

BETTER DAYS

at
VILLA STEFANO

(Kingsway, next to Holborn Tube)

ON

SATURDAY JUNE 5th

10.30 p.m. – 5.00 a.m.

D.J.s

STEVE PROCTOR

AL McKENZIE

(D/REAM)

JOHN DIGWOOD

(RENAISSANCE)

MARK RUFTON

'THIS IS A HAPPY HOUSE'
Printed by the Music Press 0850 877817

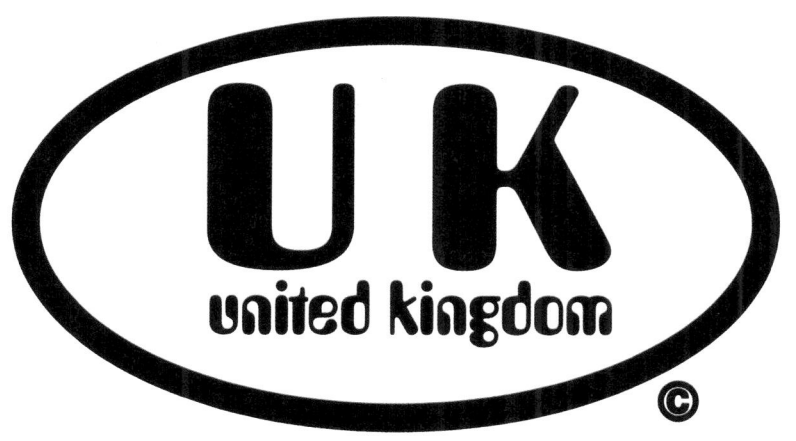

3 7 93

BRAND NEW VENUE

OPENING NIGHT
SATURDAY 3rd JULY

ANDY WEATHERALL

JUSTIN ROBERTSON

DANNY RAMPLING

FABI PARAS

ROY THE ROACH

FAT TONY

*JON THE
PLEASED WIMMIN'*

ANDY MORRIS

PAUL KELLY

BEST OF BRITISH
EVERY FRIDAY
STARTING 9th JULY

PAUL DALEY

SMOKIN' JO

ROCKY & DIESEL

*SCOTT & DANNY
MAC*

BOOT BOYS

CHRIS & JAMES

COLIN HUDD

NIC LOVEUR

*JON THE
PLEASED WIMMIN'*

3 MAIN AREAS

"It is what It is"

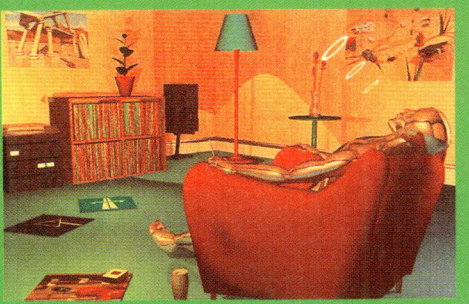

Artificial Intelligence at
The Ministry of Sound March 25/93

"It is what It is"

Warp presents

A Night of Artificial Intelligence

Live

Black Dog

DJs

Derrick May, Aphex Twin, B12
Lewis Keogh (Bandulu, The Orb), Insync
Mark Broom, Alex Knight (Fat Cat)

plus Virtual Nightclub

Thursday March 25/93 10.00pm/5.00am

£7.00 £5.00 with invite. £4.00 after 3.00am

Ticket Outlet Fatcat Records 071-497 1359

Ministry of Sound 103 Gaunt St., London SE1. 071-378 6528

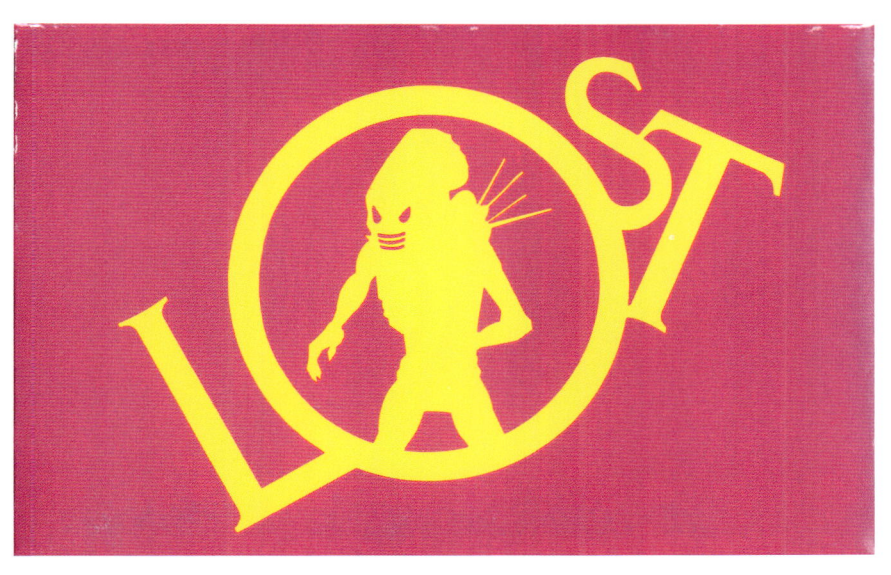

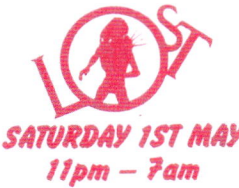

SATURDAY 1ST MAY
11pm – 7am

ROOM 1

COLIN FAVER   STEVE BICKNELL

GUESTS: DERRICK MAY
C.J. BOLLAND
LAURENT GARNIER

ROOM 2

PHIL ASHER   ANDY MARRIOTT
GLYNE BRATHWAITE   MARIO

GUEST: A.J. (SMART BOYS)

FOR TICKET INFO. P.T.O.

TICKETS AVAILABLE FROM:

APPLE, 37 SURREY ST., CROYDON

BITING BACK, PARROCK ST., GRAVESEND

CATCH A GROOVE, DEAN ST., W1

FAT CAT, MONMOUTH ST., WC2

JELLY JAM RECS., BRIGHTON & PORTSMOUTH

PLASTIC SURGERY, UNIT 16, STARNESS CRT., MAIDSTONE

QUAFF, BERWICK ST., W1

TROUBLESOME, 2 APPLE MKT., KINGSTON

VINYL SOLUTION, PORTOBELLO RD., W11

BASIC WORKS, 15, THE MARTLETS, CRAWLEY

BLACK MARKET, D'ARBLAY ST., W1

CHOCI'S CHEWNS, BOY, OLD COMPTON ST., SOHO

FLIPSIDE, 8 LAYSTALL ST., EC1

MUSIC POWER, CENTREWAY, ILFORD

PURE GROOVE, 679 HOLLOWAY RD., N19

TAG, 5 RUPERT COURT, W1

UNITY, BEAK ST., W1

ZOOM, CAMDEN HIGH ST., NW1

INFO: 071 791 0402

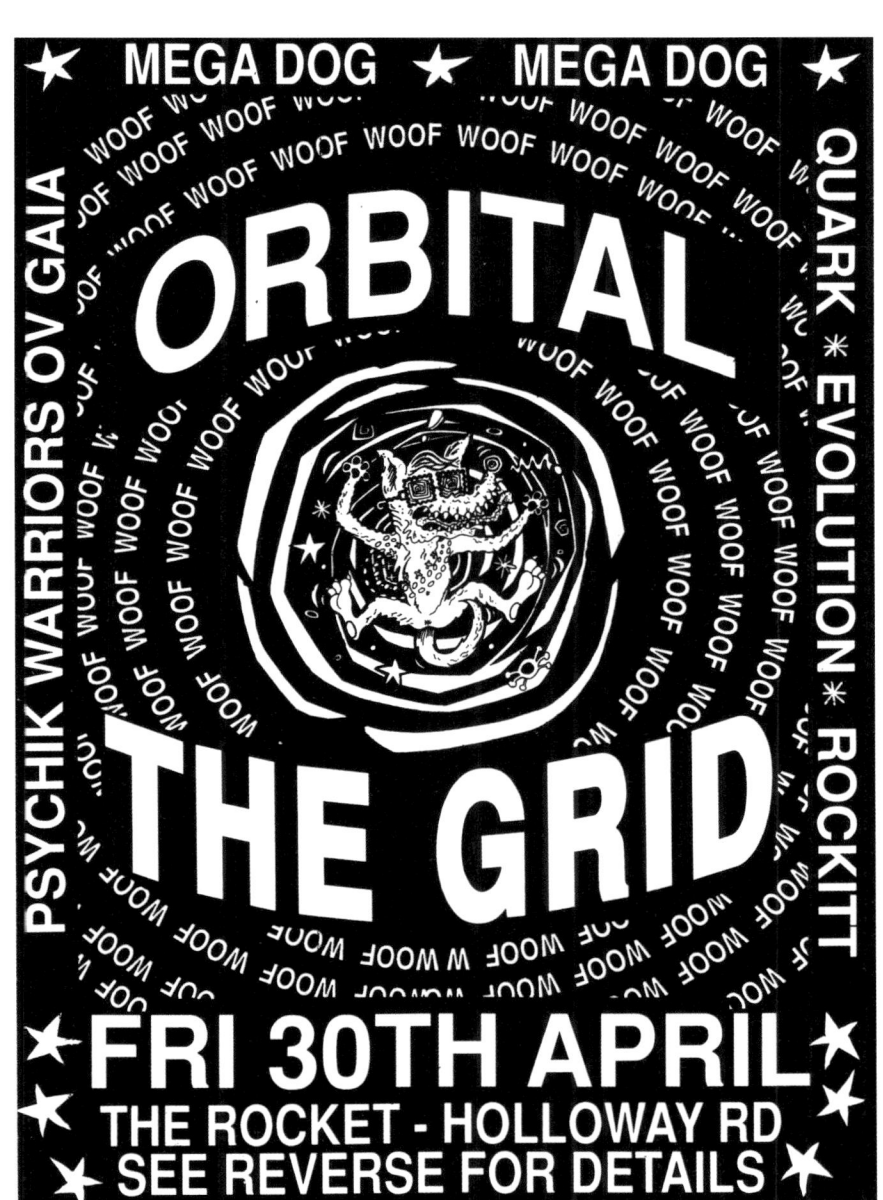

MEGA DOG ★ MEGA DOG

ORBITAL

THE GRID

PSYCHIK WARRIORS OV GAIA

QUARK ✳ EVOLUTION ✳ ROCKITT

FRI 30TH APRIL
THE ROCKET - HOLLOWAY RD
SEE REVERSE FOR DETAILS

MEGA - DOG

ALL NIGHT LIVE BAND AND D.J. SOUNDCLASH

A multi-media extravaganza, a crossover of dance sounds in two rooms with added visuals, circus games and amusements. - Be there!

ORBITAL
THE GRID
PSYCHIK WARRIORS OV GAIA

GUEST SOUNDSYSTEMS

QUARK. LIBERATOR DJS. ROCKITT. CLOGGI. JACQUES. EVOLUTION.

MICHAEL DOG & MR. BECKER.

THE ULTIMATE BRAIN BLASTING OPTICAL LIGHTSHOW BY HASSID CASUALTY, FRUIT SALAD & THE COLOUR SOUND EXPERIMENT. PLUS A THROBBING TURBO SOUND P.A. SYSTEM.

9PM - 6AM, FRI 30TH APRIL
THE ROCKET - HOLLOWAY RD N7

ADM. £10. TICKETS AVAILABLE IN ADVANCE FROM ROUGH TRADE, RHYTHM RECORDS (CAMDEN) & FAT CAT RECORDS.

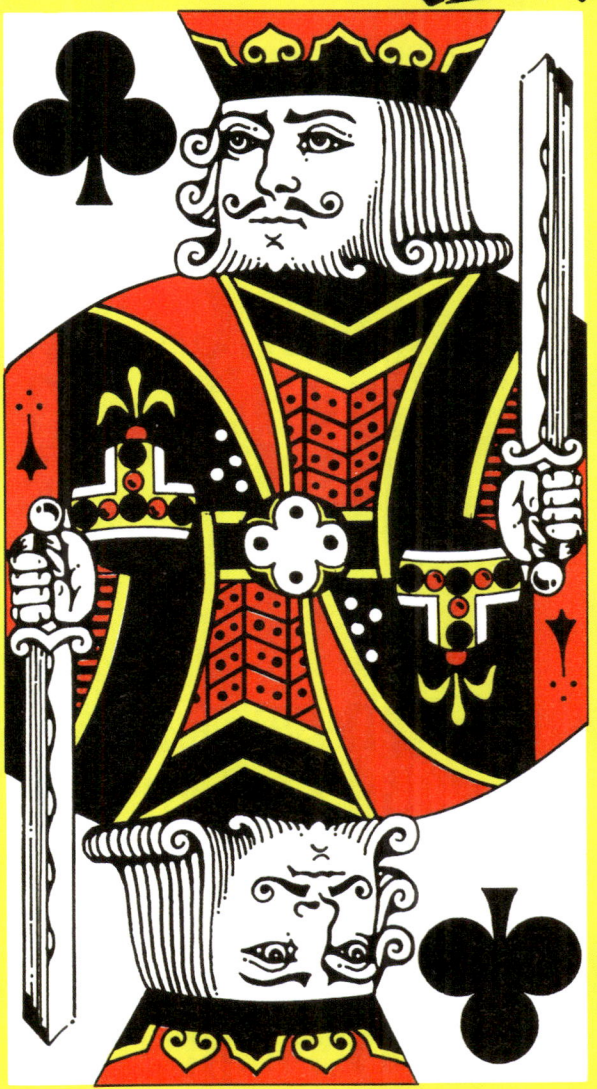

TONITE'S THE NITE IF YOU

PLAY YA CARDZ RIGHT

shuffling the Dex's

Billy nasty Steve lloyd nic love ur andy hogan brandon block a.lex.p. ginger mick robinson plus terry marks

at the king of clubs

iceni 11 white horse st, mayfair, w1. friday 2nd april £10. ten until 3.30

Dealing da card's

♣ Tag·0143400 29·zoom·0712 674 479 Bluebird·0813 133413·info·0831376974

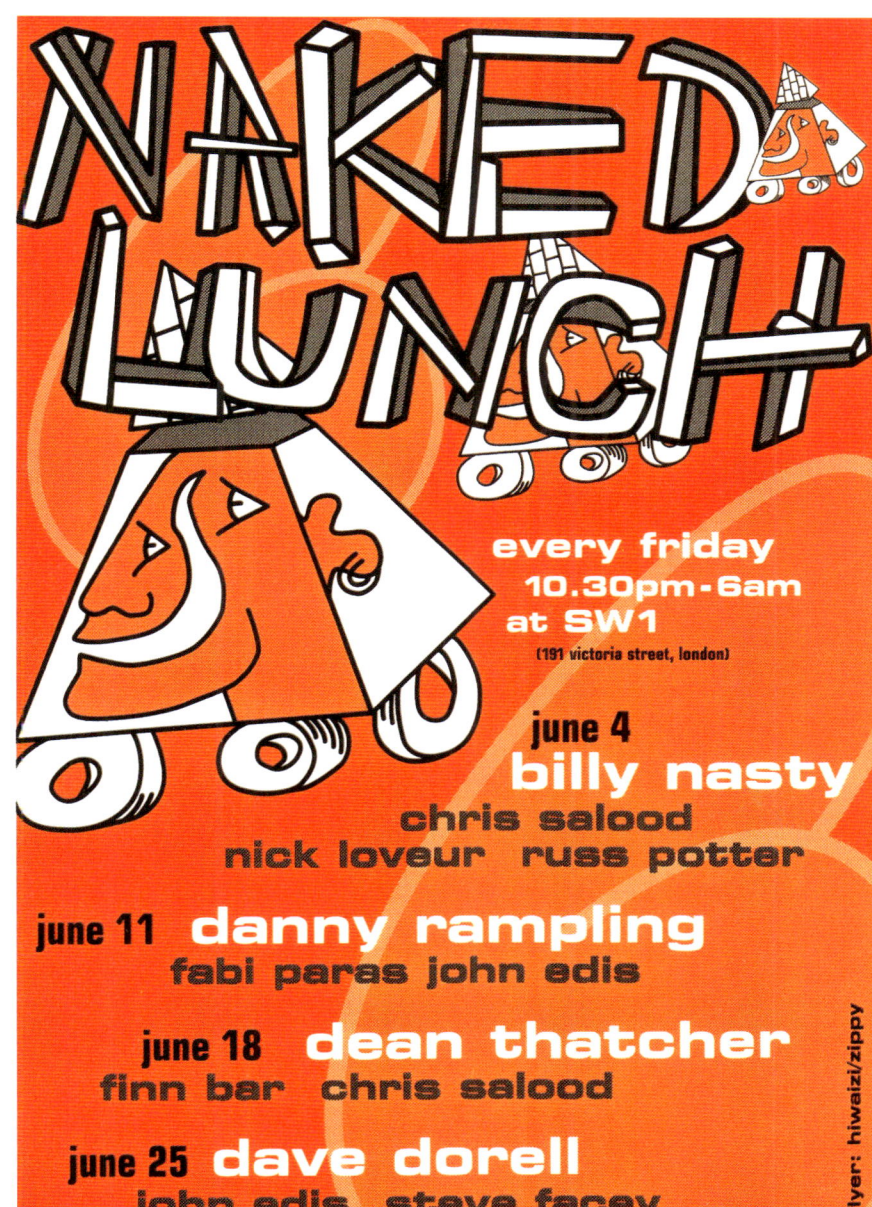

NAKED LUNCH

every friday
10.30pm-6am
at SW1
(191 victoria street, london)

june 4
billy nasty
chris salood
nick loveur   russ potter

june 11 **danny rampling**
fabi paras john edis

june 18 **dean thatcher**
finn bar chris salood

june 25 **dave dorell**
john edis steve facey

flyer: hiwaizi/zippy

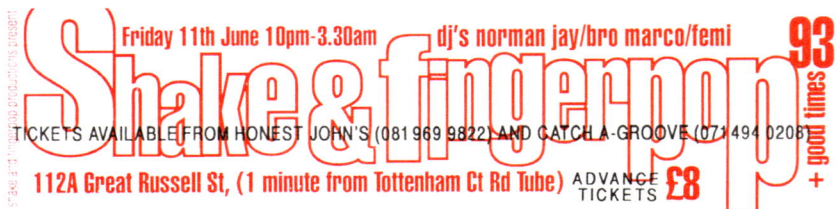

Friday 11th June 10pm-3.30am   dj's norman jay/bro marco/femi

Shake & fingerpop

93

+ good times

TICKETS AVAILABLE FROM HONEST JOHN'S (081 969 9822) AND CATCH-A-GROOVE (071 494 0208)

112A Great Russell St, (1 minute from Tottenham Ct Rd Tube)   ADVANCE TICKETS £8

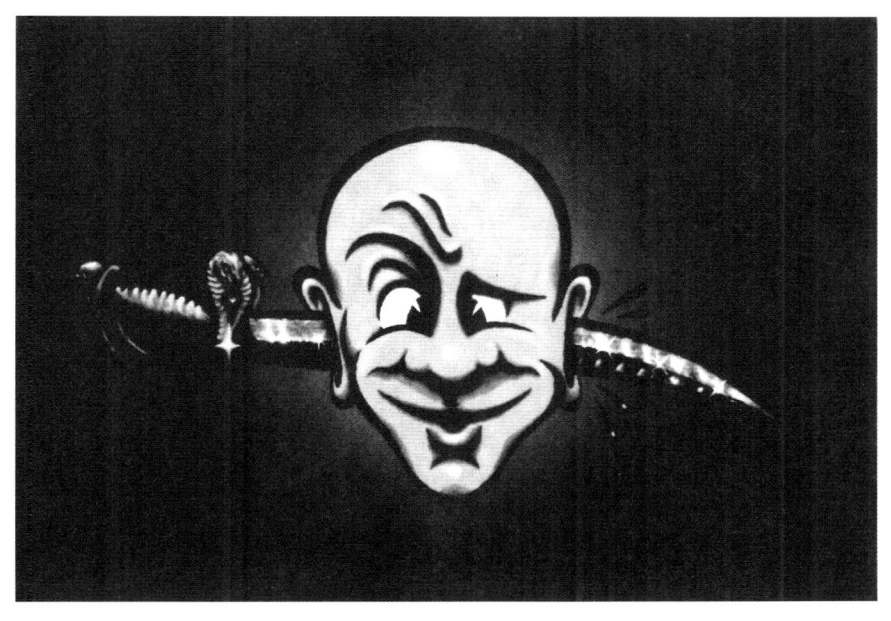

SABRESONIC

ROUNDING UP NINETEEN NINETY THREE...
...THE MOODSWINGS CONTINUE!

FRI NOV 26th: ANDREW WEATHERALL WARMING UP FOR, TWITCH & BRAINSTORM (DJ's FROM WHAT,...IN LORD SABRE'S HUMBLE OPINION, IS THE FINEST CLUB IN THE U.K. "PURE IN EDINBURGH"...)

FRI DEC 3rd: DOMINIC MOIR WARMS UP FOR LORD SABRE WITH A "DEEP HOUSE & OLD SCHOOL DETROIT DROP NICE SESSION"...

FRI DEC 10th: NEIL BARNES & PAUL DALEY (LEFTFIELD TAKE OVER THE SABRESONIC TWIN RADIOGRAMS FOR THE FULL 5½ HOURS!...)

FRI DEC 17th: SABRESONIC PAGAN CHRIST-MAS PARTY...DETAILS WILL INDEED FOLLOW.

Happy Jax, Arch 5, Crucifix Lane, S.E.1
9pm—2.30am. Members £5 Non-members £6

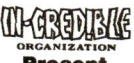

ORGANIZATION

Present

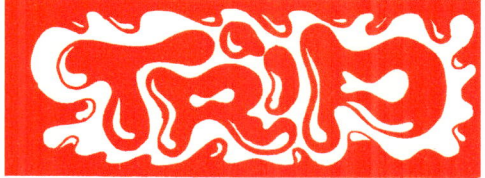

and

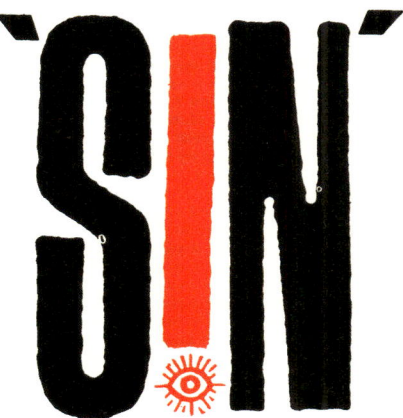

A

P
A
R
T

1

'FLASHBACK'

A night of Acid House, Balearic Beats and records that warped a whole generation

P
A
R
T

1

Boxing Day Dec. 26th

(Bank Hol. next day) 10pm 'til 6am

London Astoria,

157 Charing Cross Rd W1

071 434 9592

DJs:

PAUL OAKENFOLD

NICKY HOLLOWAY

PETE TONG

ALFREDO

JAZZY M

FAT TONY

COLIN HUDD

'Turn on tune in and get right on one matey'

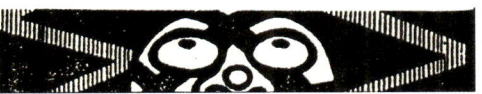

TRIP started at the end of May 1988 and was the first BIG Saturday House and Balearic night in London if not the country. Due to adverse publicity that other clubs were attracting at the time it changed it's name to SIN in January 89. Sin ran for a couple of years before handing over to the Crazy club who pushed the night into more of a Hardcore situation.

It was the first place David Morales played in this country and was also instrumental in launching the careers of such people as Andy Weatherall and Fabi Paras (who used to play there) M. People's front man Mike Pickering played on the opening night and over the years our stage was graced by just about everyone around at the time.

Many of todays clubbers will admit to having their first 'Experience' at TRIP and judging by the reaction we have had from our friends all the old faces will be coming out of the woodwork for a little bit of a reunion, the average age at TRIP/SIN was about 20 at the time and it will be funny to see what everyone is up to now they're 25 plus.

This night is a complete one off that has been planned to happen for months and months-well before the recent events of this type and will never be done again. If you never used to attend why not come along and find out what you missed. It's not a closed shop and you are more than welcome. The only thing you need to bring is a ticket and a big smile!

TICKETS £20 IN ADVANCE
£25 ON THE NIGHT IF AVAILABLE
(Unlikely)

Available from the following outlets:
INNER LONDON:
THE ASTORIA, SOHO - 071 434 0403
TAG RECORDS, SOHO - 071 434 0029
BLACK MARKET, SOHO - 071 437 0478
SIGN OF THE TIMES , COVENT GDN, 071 240 7366
FLYING RECORDS, KENSINGTON - 071 938 4407
VINYL ZONE, FULHAM - 071 384 2320
DISPENSARY, NOTTING HILL - 071 221 9290
QUAFF RECORDS, SOHO - 071 734 4152
ZOOM RECORDS, CAMDEN - 071 267 4479
PARADOX, ISLINGTON - 071 226 8530
OUTER LONDON:
POUR HOMME,WELLING - 081 301 1625
BEGGARS BANQUET, KINGSTON - 081 549 5871
SLOUGH RECORDS, SLOUGH - 0753 526194
VINYL MANIA, EALING - 081 566 5244
APPLE RECORDS, CROYDON -081 686 8786
BLUEBIRD RECORDS, BROMLEY - 081 313 3413
RECORD & DISCO CENTRE, RAYNERS LANE - 081 868 8637
IAN ELLIS, ESSEX - 0708 736592

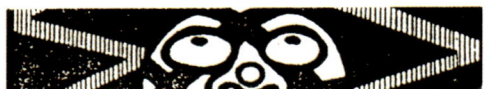

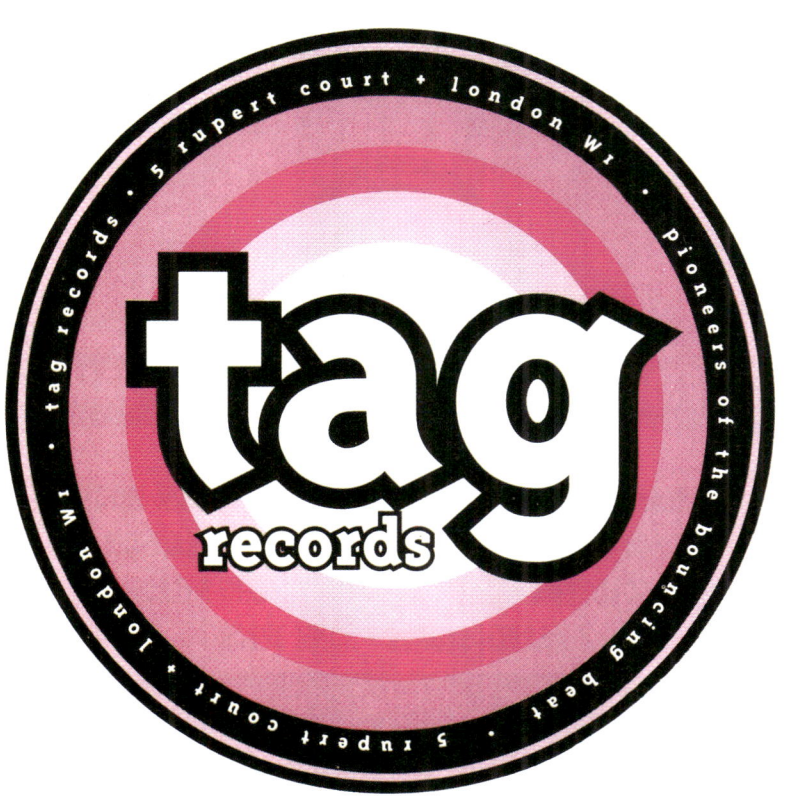

tag records · 5 rupert court · london w1 · pioneers of the bouncing beat · 5 rupert court · london w1 · tag records

tag
records

BEST OF BRITISH

— M E E T S —

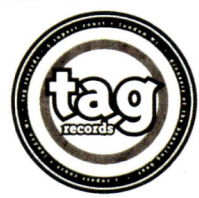

FRIDAY 27TH AUGUST · 10PM TIL 6AM

D J's

- DARREN EMMERSON · DANNY RAMPLING · MARK MOORE ·
- · SMOKIN JO · LAURENCE NELSON · SIMON HANSON ·
- · NIC LOVEUR · CRAIG CAMPBELL · JOHN NELSON ·
- · DARREN STOKES · JOHN BEECH ·

Admission £10 · Members £8 · £6 after 3am

UK · Buckhold Road, Wandsworth, London SW18

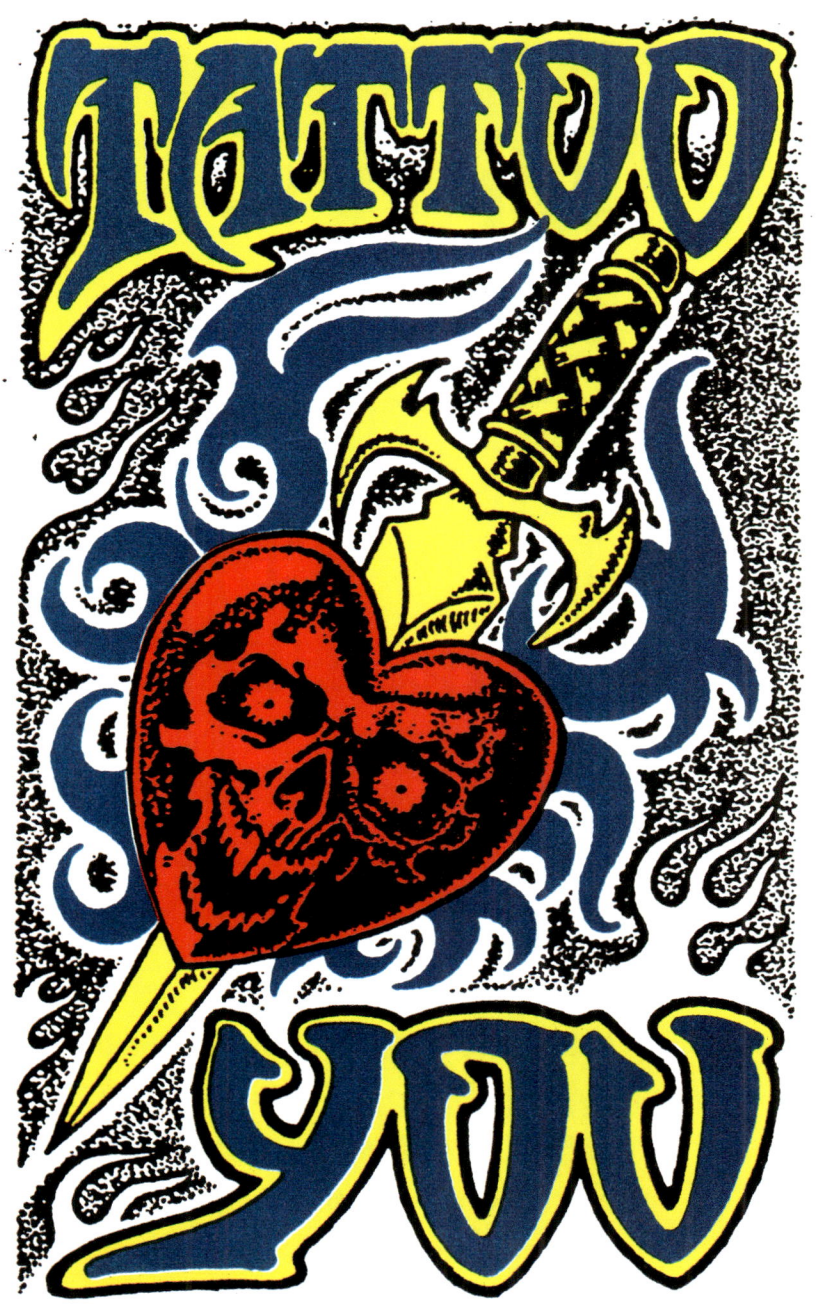

SUICIDE SHIFT PRESENTS

TATTOO
YOU

SUICIDE SHIFT PRESENTS

TATTOO YOU

DJ'S
DANNY RAMPLING
DARREN EMERSON
PAUL DALEY
RAD RICE
AND
ANDY WEATHERALL

PLUS PLAYING LIVE DOWNSTAIRS IN THE ROCK CELLAR

THE DISCO ASSASSINS,
TRAFALGAR, T1000,
ALL NEW ACCELERATORS,

PLUS FROM THE USA SPECIAL GUESTS

NAKED TRUTH

WITH DISCO ASSASSINS DJ'S AND ANDY WEATHERALL.

SATURDAY 13TH MARCH, 10PM – 6AM.

CENTRAL LONDON VENUE

TICKETS FROM QUAFF RECORDS, BERWICK STREET W1,
TAG RECORDS, RUPERT COURT W1, SIGN OF THE TIMES, KEN MARKET,
FLYING RECORDS, KEN MARKET.

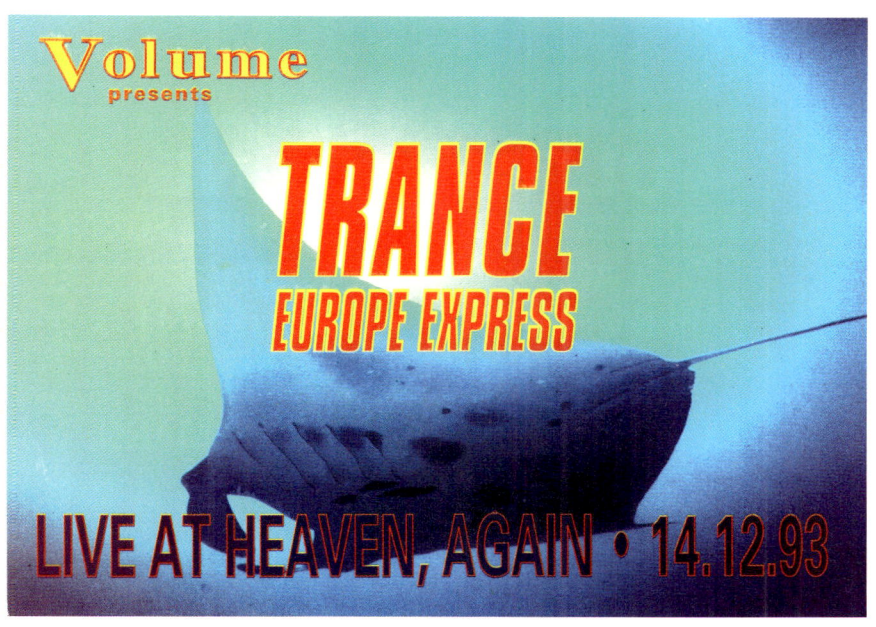

LIVE AT HEAVEN, AGAIN

TUESDAY DECEMBER 14 1993 • 10.00pm - 3.30am
HEAVEN • VILLIERS ST • LONDON WC2

LIVE: **ULTRAMARINE**

HIGHER INTELLIGENCE AGENCY • AUTECHRE • RELOAD

DJs: **ANDREW WEATHERALL**

DARREN EMERSON • CHARLIE HALL

EGON ZO • SHERMAN AT THE CONTROLS • KRIS NEEDS

AMBIENT ROOM:

ALEX PATERSON & THOMAS FEHLMANN

TICKETS £10 FROM: FLYING RECORDS/SIGN OF THE TIMES (Kensington Market), ROUGH TRADE (Talbot Rd/Neals Yd),
FAT CAT (Monmouth St), TAG RECORDS (Rupert Ct), SISTER RAY (Berwick St), or by post from VOLUME: 071 706 8122

TRANCE EUROPE EXPRESS: A Volume Special Edition – 2 CDs, 192-page full colour book, 24 exclusive tracks from top pop acts
The Orb, Orbital, The Aphex Twin, Sabres Of Paradise, System 7, CJ Bolland, Moby, Black Dog, Cosmic Baby,
The Drum Club, Sven Väth, Psychick Warriors Ov Gaia, The Source, and more. Available at great record shops.

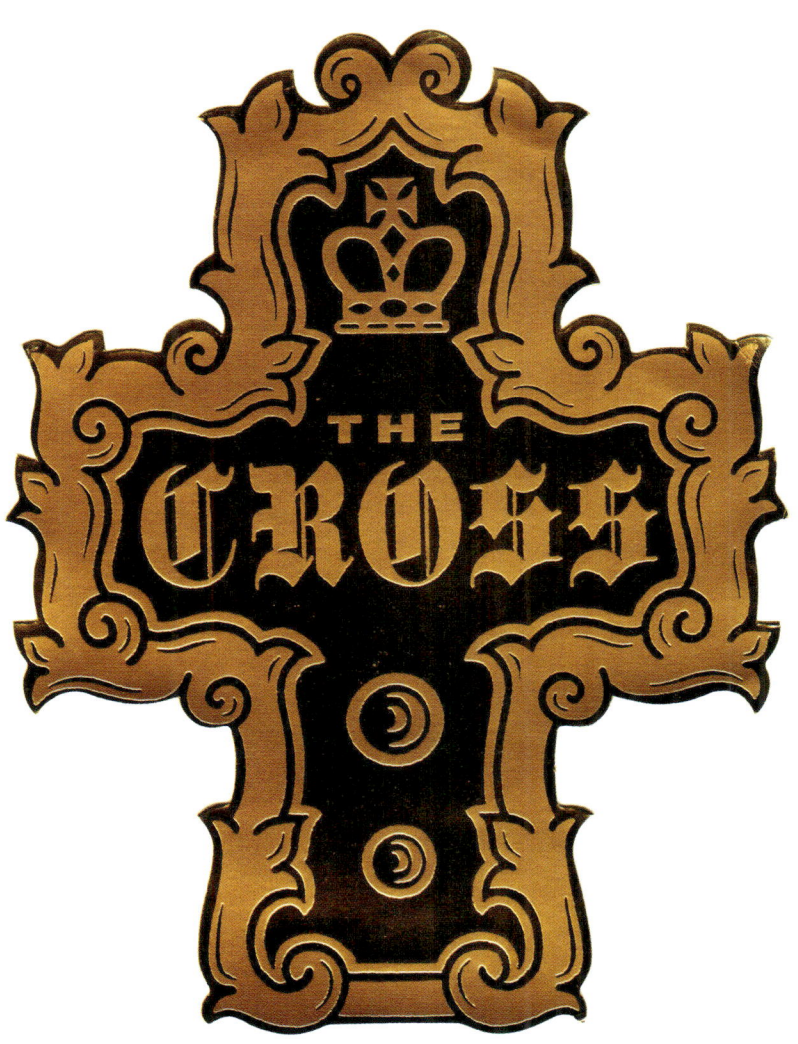

PARTAKE

IN A NIGHT OF

HEAVENLY TUNES

AND DIVINE

INSPIRATION

INDULGE YOURSELF

SUBMIT TO

INTEMPERANCE

FRIDAY 5TH NOVEMBER
9.30PM TILL 4AM
THE CROSS
KINGS CROSS GOODS YARD
YORK WAY
KINGS CROSS N1 0BB

STRICTLY INVITE ONLY
ADMITS ONE
☎
071 837 0828

EVERY THURSDAY

FROM JAN 6th 1994

£6/£3 MEMBERS CONCS
£3 B4 10pm

9.30pm - 3am
INFO LINE
081 450 4508

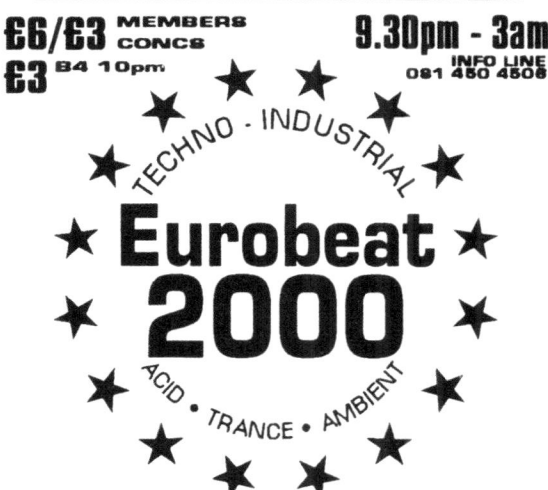

TECHNO · INDUSTRIAL

Eurobeat 2000

ACID · TRANCE · AMBIENT

THE GENUINE ARTICLE

RESIDENT DJs

DAVE CLARKE · T23
ALEX HAZZARD · FRANKIE D
THE DENTIST · OPEN MIND

GUEST DJs (MIN 2 PER NIGHT)

DAVE ANGEL · WARLOCK
MIXMASTER MORRIS
LENNY DEE · RICHARD NORRIS
(THE GRID)
G.T.O · COLIN DALE · EON
COLIN FAVER · DAZ SAUND

THE LIMELIGHT
136 SHAFTESBURY AVE. LONDON W1

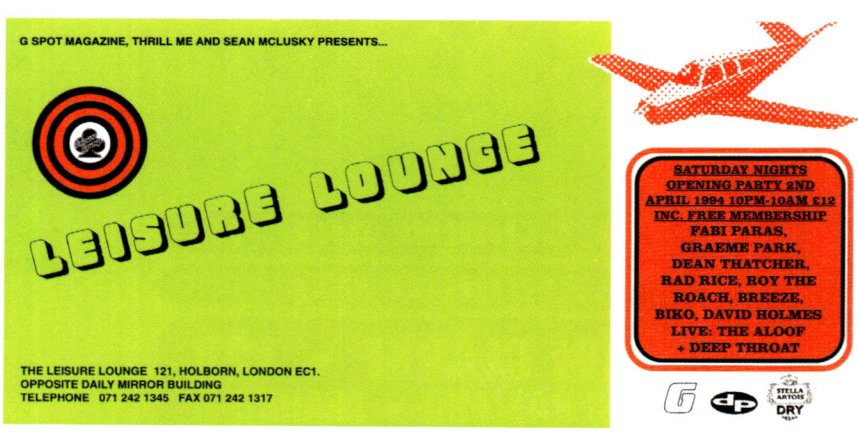

G SPOT MAGAZINE, THRILL ME AND SEAN MCLUSKY PRESENTS...

LEISURE LOUNGE

THE LEISURE LOUNGE 121, HOLBORN, LONDON EC1.
OPPOSITE DAILY MIRROR BUILDING
TELEPHONE 071 242 1345 FAX 071 242 1317

SATURDAY NIGHTS
OPENING PARTY 2ND
APRIL 1994 10PM-10AM £12
INC. FREE MEMBERSHIP
FABI PARAS,
GRAEME PARK,
DEAN THATCHER,
RAD RICE, ROY THE
ROACH, BREEZE,
BIKO, DAVID HOLMES
LIVE: THE ALOOF
+ DEEP THROAT

STELLA
ARTOIS
DRY

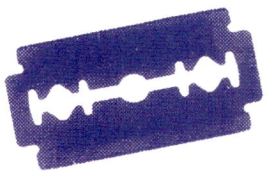

ICONELASTIC

Every Wednesday
10.30 - 3.30am

Club Koo
Leicester Square
(next to odeon cinema)

Wednesday April

Fabi Paras
Paul Langley   Haje

and in the cinema lounge...

Mixmaster Morris
Bongo

£5

OUTHAUS PRODUCTS · 1 CUTLERS TERRACE BALLS POND ROAD N1 · 071 275 9278 · ICONELASTIC

I KNOW THE DI

luvdup

LUVDUP AT VELVET UNDERGROUND
143 CHARING CROSS RD LONDON W1
10.00 TILL 4.00/ADMISSION £6.00
INFO 061-237 3710/071-439 4655
THURSDAY 17 FEBRUARY
DJS ADRIAN AND MARK LUVDUP
GUEST KELVIN ANDREWS (GOLDEN)

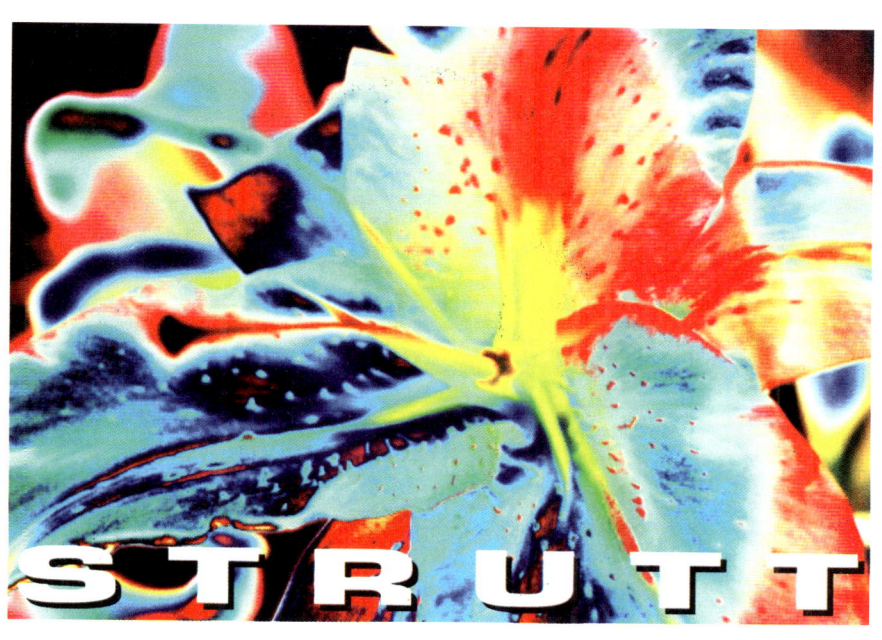

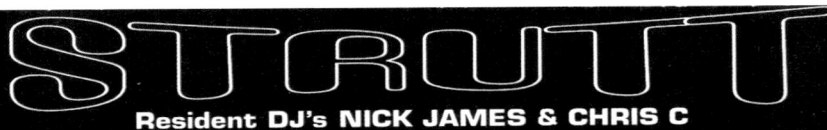

STRUTT

Resident DJ's NICK JAMES & CHRIS C

FABIO PARAS Nov 20th
BILLY NASTY Nov 27th
MIKE MAGUIRE (Juno Reactor) Dec 4th
ANDREW WEATHERALL (3hr set) Dec 11th

RICHIE HAWTIN Dec 18th · 3hr set · 2am extension · £7

BOXING DAY SPECIAL Mon 26th Dec
DERRICK MAY, EDDIE RICHARDS
STEVE HOLISTIC and Residents 10pm-6am @ The Cross £14

STRUTT DELUXE IV - NEW YEARS EVE PARTY
ALEX KNIGHT, FABIO PARAS, PAUL DALEY, BILLY NASTY
VAN BASTEN IN DUB, STEVE HOLISTIC and Residents Sat 31st Dec
9.30pm-6am Central London Location £18 adv from Strutt, or £23 @
Fat Cat, Zoom, Flying, Beggars, Tag, The George. Info 081 964 3172

Strutt will then take a break re-opening with Garnier on Feb 26th
£5 Every Sunday 8pm-1am The Cross, Goods Yard, Kings Cross N1

Art & Design Buggy G. Riphead

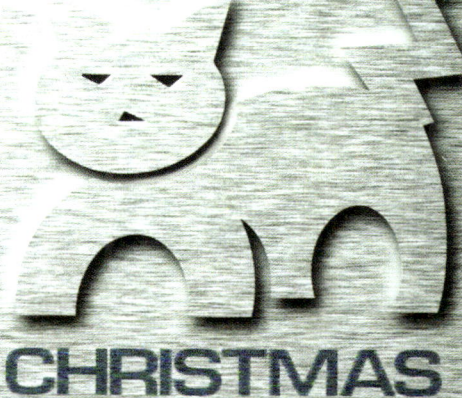

CHRISTMAS PARTY

PLAID – LIVE	**SATURDAY**
	16:12:95
STEVE BICKNELL	
MARK BROOM	
ALEX KNIGHT	
LEE GRAINGE	
JOHN REYNOLDS	
DAVE BROOK	
RICHARD THOMAS	

**ADMISSION BY
INVITE ONLY**

INVITES ONLY AVAILABLE FROM 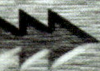 FATCAT

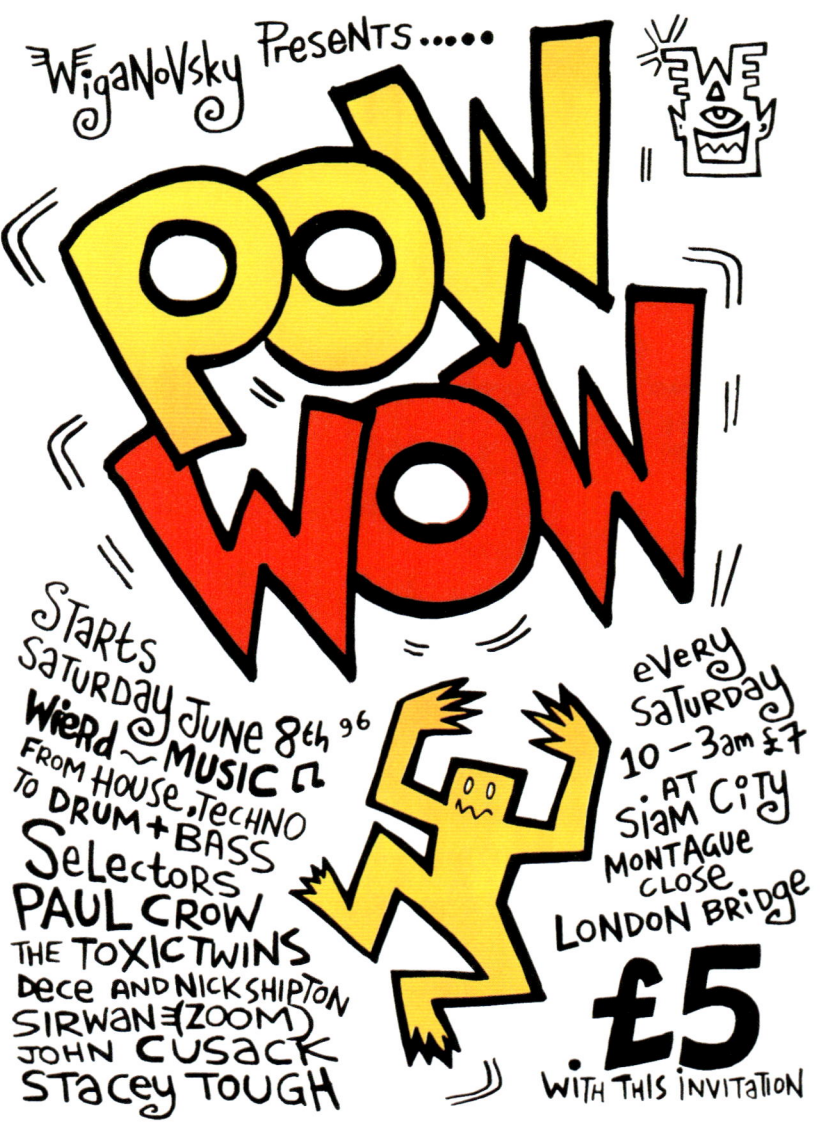

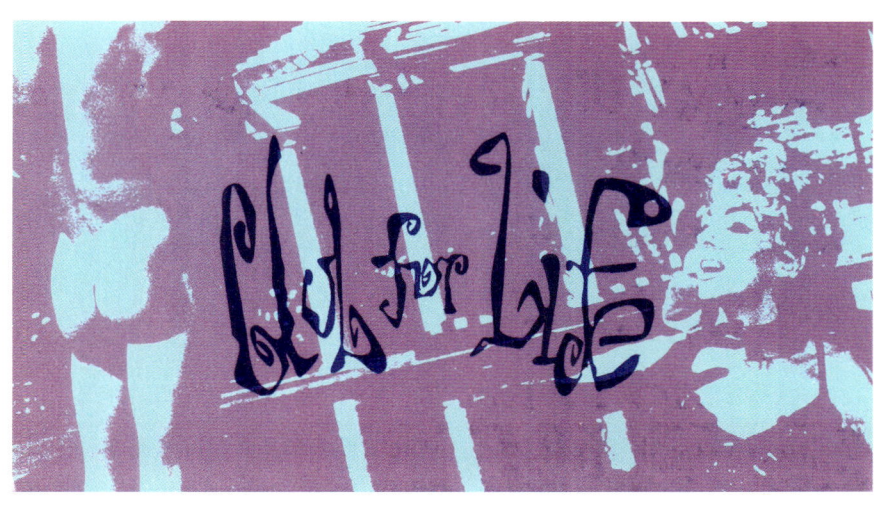

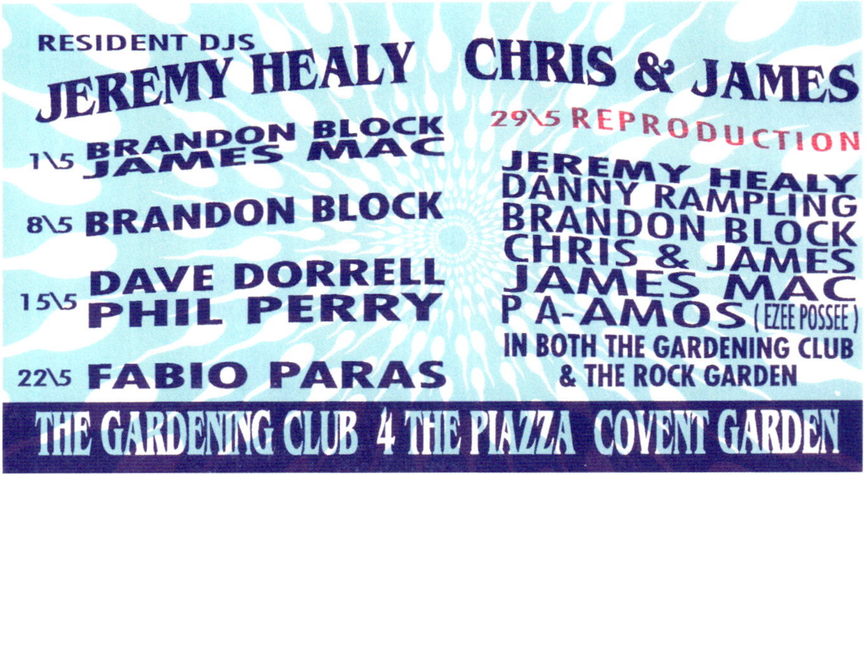

RESIDENT DJS
JEREMY HEALY CHRIS & JAMES
1\5 BRANDON BLOCK JAMES MAC
8\5 BRANDON BLOCK
15\5 DAVE DORRELL PHIL PERRY
22\5 FABIO PARAS
29\5 REPRODUCTION
JEREMY HEALY
DANNY RAMPLING
BRANDON BLOCK
CHRIS & JAMES
JAMES MAC
P A-AMOS (EZEE POSSEE)
IN BOTH THE GARDENING CLUB & THE ROCK GARDEN
THE GARDENING CLUB 4 THE PIAZZA COVENT GARDEN

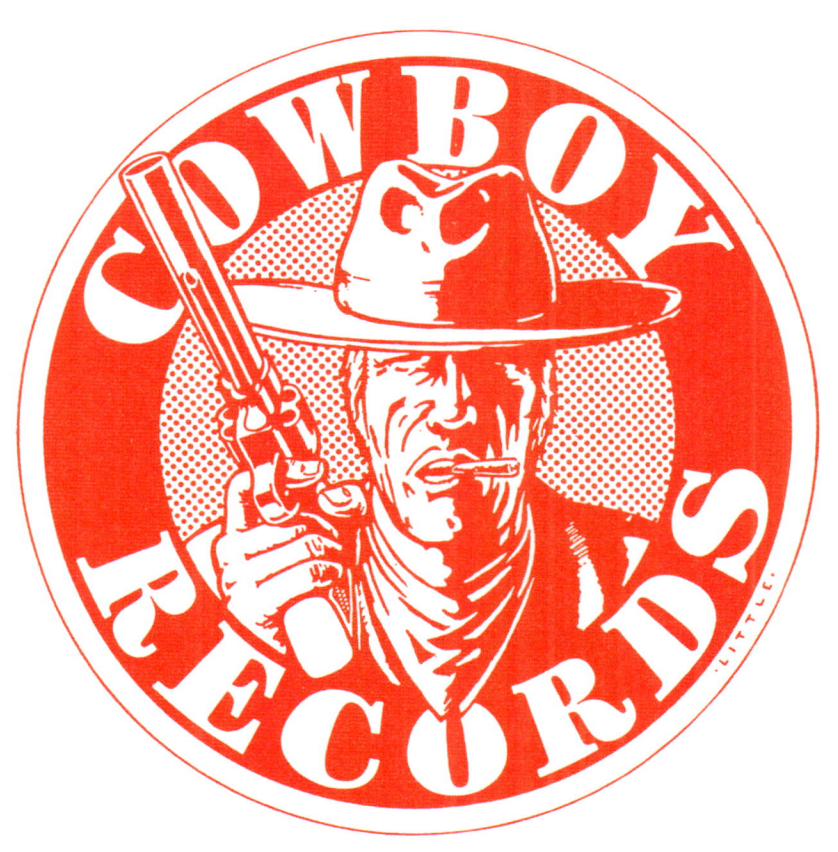

Cowboy Records

Present

SECRET

LIFE

ONSTAGE

Plus djs

Terry Farley

Pete Heller

Clive Henry

FRI. JAN. 22

10–3

£8 in advance
£10 on the night

Tickets from:
'Flying Records,'
Kensington Mkt.
'Milk Bar,' 12 Sutton Row W1

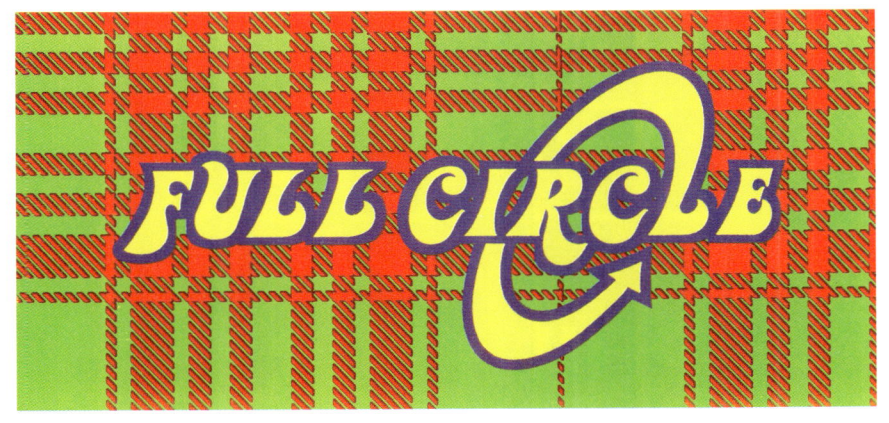

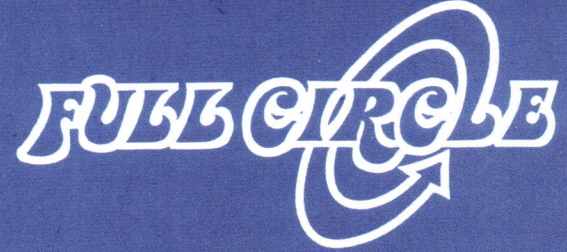

FULL CIRCLE

BOXING DAY BEANO!

WITH

PHIL PERRY
FABI PARAS
CLIVE HENRY
ROCKY & DIESEL

4PM TILL MIDNIGHT
£10 ON DOOR
ARRIVE EARLY !

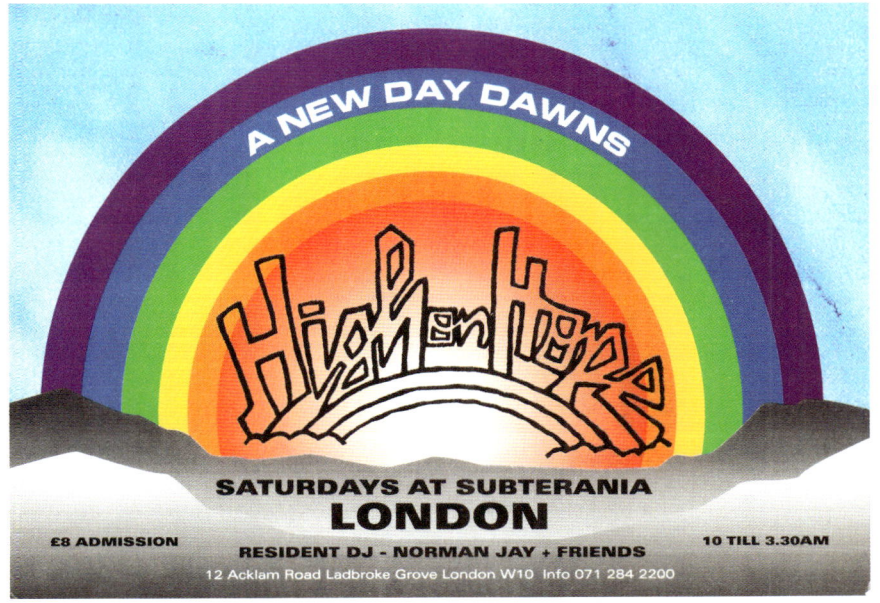

A NEW DAY DAWNS

High on Hope

SATURDAYS AT SUBTERANIA
LONDON

£8 ADMISSION   RESIDENT DJ - NORMAN JAY + FRIENDS   10 TILL 3.30AM

12 Acklam Road Ladbroke Grove London W10 Info 071 284 2200

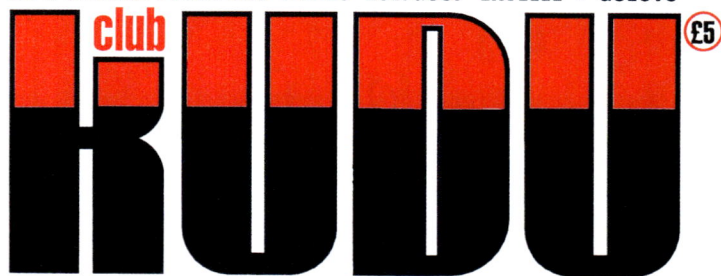

DJ'S PATRICK FORGE AND JAMES 'HOLYGOOF' LAVELLE + GUESTS

club KUDU £5

EVERY THURSDAY AT THE GARDENING CLUB (4 THE PIAZZA, COVENT GARDEN, W2) 10PM TILL 3.30

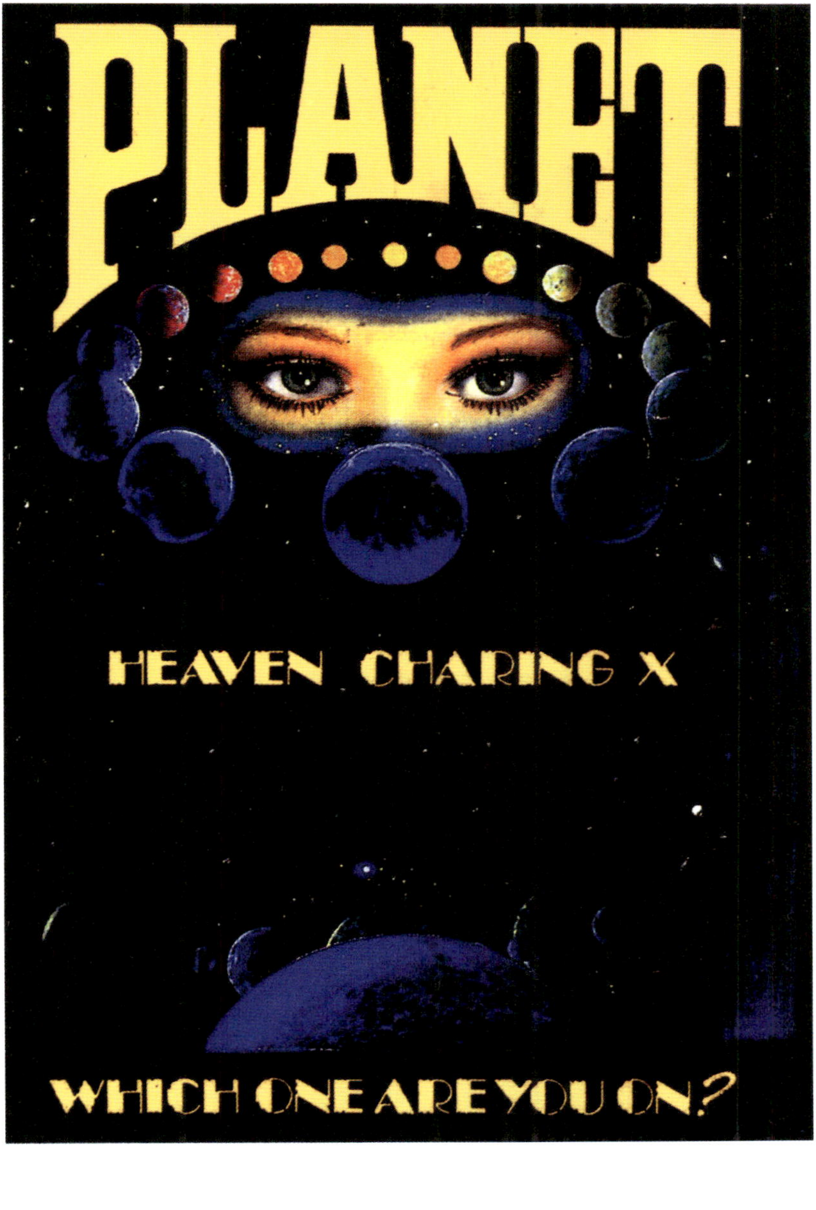
PLANET
HEAVEN CHARING X
WHICH ONE ARE YOU ON?

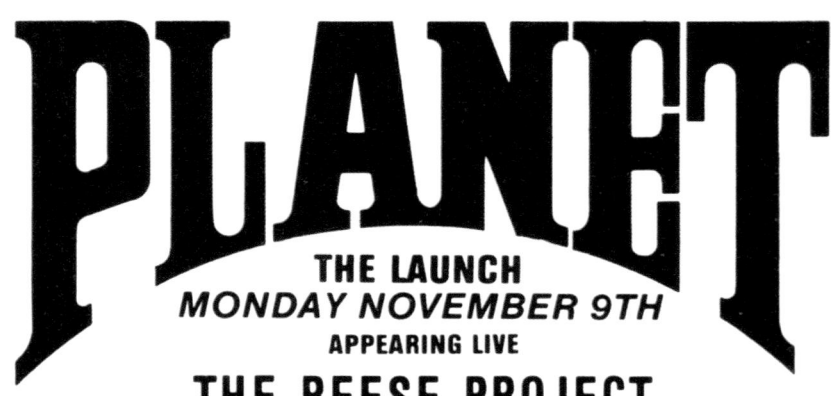

PLANET

THE LAUNCH
MONDAY NOVEMBER 9TH
APPEARING LIVE

THE REESE PROJECT
(DIRECT ME, I BELIEVE, THE COLOR OF LOVE)

ALYS-ONE
(FOLLOW-ME)

CHEZ DAMIER
(CAN YOU FEEL IT)

UNIVERSAL SOUNDS BY

KEVIN SAUNDERSON
(DETROIT)

DARREN EMERSON
KID BATCHELOR
LINDEN C
RICKY MORRISON

LUNA BAR
ROY THE ROACH
TOMMY D
CHOCOLATE FUDGE

SPACE BAR
ABBEY
MATTHEW WHITEHEAD

LONDON
EVERY MONDAY - HEAVEN - CHARING X
10.30 - 3.30 - ENTRANCE £5.00
CONCEPT BY C.P.O. • LONDON • 1992©

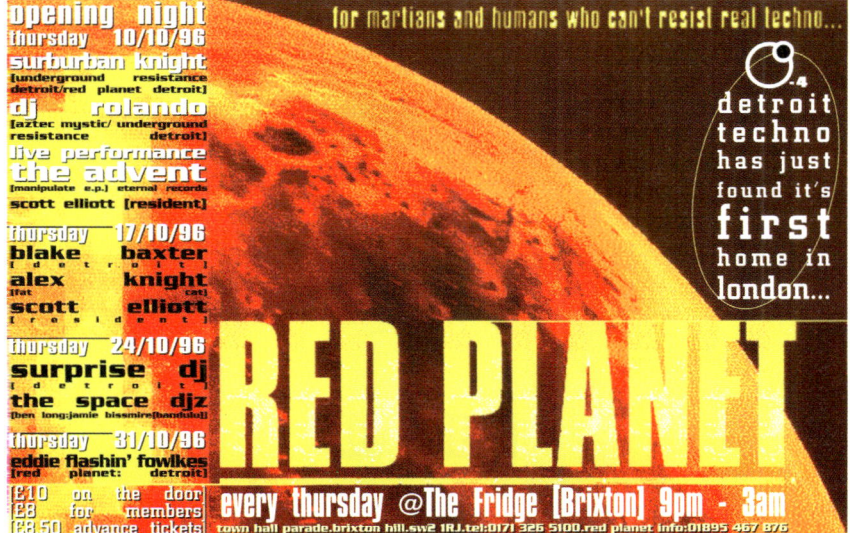

for martians and humans who can't resist real techno...

opening night
thursday 10/10/96
surburban knight
[underground resistance detroit/red planet detroit]
dj rolando
[aztec mystic/ underground resistance detroit]
live performance
the advent
[manipulate e.p.] eternal records
scott elliott [resident]

thursday 17/10/96
blake baxter
[detroit]
alex knight
[fat cat]
scott elliott
[resident]

thursday 24/10/96
surprise dj
[detroit]
the space djz
[ben long;jamie bissmire(bandulu)]

thursday 31/10/96
eddie flashin' fowlkes
[red planet: detroit]

[£10 on the door]
[£8 for members]
[£8.50 advance tickets]

detroit
techno
has just
found it's
first
home in
london...

RED PLANET

every thursday @The Fridge [Brixton] 9pm - 3am
town hall parade.brixton hill.sw2 1RJ.tel:0171 326 5100.red planet info:01895 467 876

Saturday December 7th
The End's 1st Birthday

Derrick May
Darren Emerson
Cajmere
Satoshi Tomiie
Layo
Mr C

Tickets £20 in advance only

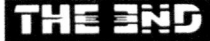

16a West Central St WC1